A
GROSSET
ALL-COLOR GUIDE

DISCOVERY OF NORTH AMERICA

BY MICHÈLE BYAM
Illustrated by G. J. Galsworthy

GROSSET & DUNLAP
A NATIONAL GENERAL COMPANY
Publishers ▪ New York

THE GROSSET ALL-COLOR GUIDE SERIES
SUPERVISING EDITOR . . . GEORG ZAPPLER

Board of Consultants

RICHARD G. VAN GELDER · Chairman and Curator, Mammals, American Museum of Natural History

WILLIAM C. STEERE · Director, New York Botanical Garden

SUNE ENGELBREKTSON · Space Science Co-ordinator, Port Chester Public Schools

JOHN F. MIDDLETON · Chairman, Anthropology, New York University

CARL M. KORTEPETER · Associate Professor, History, New York University

MICHAEL COHN · Curator, Cultural History, Brooklyn Children's Museum

FRANK X. CRITCHLOW · Consulting Engineer, Applied and Theoretical Electronics

Copyright © 1972 by Grosset & Dunlap, Inc.

All Rights Reserved

Published Simultaneously in Canada

Copyright © 1970 by the Hamlyn Publishing Group Ltd.

Library of Congress Catalog Card No.: 73-154857

Printed in the United States of America

ISBN: 0-448-00883-1 (Trade Edition)

ISBN: 0-448-04173-1 (Library Edition)

CONTENTS

The first settlers in America were a Mongoloid people who came from Asia to Alaska.

From the Indians to the Norsemen to Columbus

The first man appears to have arrived in North America nearly 20,000 years ago. During the Ice Age the Bering Strait which separates North America from Asia was entirely frozen over. Men must have crossed the ice in search of food or to escape from hostile tribes, liked the area, and stayed. The descendants of these early travelers had no chance to return to Asia, for over the centuries the Ice Age glacier gradually melted, filling the seas with water once again.

The first settlers slowly moved south through Alaska and Canada, east to the Great Lakes and the Atlantic coast and some even continued as far as Central and South America. In time they populated and adapted to both the Northern and Southern Hemispheres. These first Americans came to be termed 'Indians'. Gradually these Indians became farmers as well as hunters, developing many vegetables, such as corn, beans, squash, pumpkin and potatoes, all unknown to Europe at that time. They also grew the first tobacco.

The Norsemen, primitive by even medieval standards, landed on the northern continent in about A.D. 1000. Though they left no trace in 'Vinland' of their journey there, they chronicled their exploits in 'sagas'. Some of these recount the adventures of men like Eric the Red, Bjarni Heriufson and Leif Ericson. It is only in recent years that historians have discovered that the sagas are not merely Viking legends and that the Norsemen did in fact land on the east coast of North America many times during the tenth and eleventh centuries.

Bjarni's father had sailed with Eric the Red when he colonized Greenland and in the same year—probably about A.D. 986—Bjarni sailed to meet him. He was blown off course by a violent storm and found himself, days later, off a strange coast. Unlike Greenland, it was neither mountainous, nor covered in snow. Bjarni still intended to get to Greenland, so he resisted the crew's demand that they disembark.

The routes of the Mongols and the Norsemen

Pacific Ocean

Atlantic Ocean

Mongols

Vikings

5

Leif Ericson, the Norse discoverer of America

The land which Bjarni refused to land on was North America, and it was Leif Ericson, the son of Eric the Red, in about A.D. 1000, who became the first European to land on it.

Leif got there by sailing from Greenland, thus making Bjarni's voyage in reverse. The first place he saw he christened *Helluland,* or 'Land of Flat Stone', which we now know to have been Baffin Land, north of Labrador. Traveling south and east he came to what he called *Markland,* 'Land of Woods'. During these travels, he was actually following the coasts of both Labrador and Newfoundland which he believed to be one.

The Norsemen then disembarked on a beautiful coast with miles of silver sand. This was very different land to that settled in Greenland. The Norsemen at first decided to remain for just a few days, but they stayed all autumn and winter. Almost immediately, they found grapes.

In the spring the Norsemen sailed back with a cargo of grapes and wood, to Greenland. Leif had given the land a name according to its resources, calling it *Vinland*, Land of Vines.

That the Norsemen were the first discoverers of North America is indubitable but not significant in the history of the continent as they failed to stay and colonize the land. The next important expedition had to wait for nearly 500 years until, in the Age of Discovery, man was to stretch his abilities and imagination into the unknown world across the oceans.

These voyages became possible to Europeans in the late Middle Ages by the development of the compass and the astrolabe and the gradual improvement in the structural design and building of ships that enabled them to sail against

A Viking church in Greenland as it looks today

the wind and withstand long voyages. These practical skills were allied with advances in astronomy, geography and mathematics to make navigation easier for the ordinary sea captain. However, a strong curiosity was the main force that drove such men as Portuguese explorers Bartolomeu Dias and Vasco da Gama to navigate routes first around the Cape of Good Hope and then to India.

In this age of epic voyages, the successful voyage of Christopher Columbus is the most significant. After 1492 the center of the world gradually shifted from the Mediterranean to the Atlantic.

Yet when Columbus discovered several islands off the coast of America he was actually looking for a shorter route to the riches in the Indies, and after having found this vast land mass explorers spent the next 50 years trying to get around it. For Columbus like many of his contemporaries, was not trying to find a new world but rather to find a more direct route to the old—or what we know today as the Far East.

The explorer was born Cristofero Colombo in the city of Genoa, Italy, but he settled in Portugal after being washed ashore there during a sea battle when he was 26 years old. He made several voyages under the Portuguese flag to Africa, the Madeiras and Azores. But his dream was to sail over the edge of the known world and find a new route to the Indies. To this end he absorbed all the information he could pick up about the journeys of other mariners. His plan was quite simple; he would sail to the Canary Islands and then carry on due west along latitude 28° N, which he had calculated would take his ship to Japan. Having carefully planned his voyage he first sought the patronage he needed at the Portuguese court.

But the Portuguese were not sympathetic to his ideas of carrying Christianity to the Indies and returning with gold and the other treasures for which the Orient had become legendary. Today, indeed, one can say that Columbus' critics were more practical than he was. For neither he nor

Christopher Columbus with Martin Behaim's globe of 1492—it showed an unbroken stretch of ocean from Europe to Asia.

SHIPBUILDING IN THE 15th CENTURY

they knew that there was a large continent between Europe and Asia, and if that continent had not existed Columbus would have had to sail a distance of 10,000 miles over an empty ocean and then journey back—a virtually impossible task for seamen and ships of that time.

Undeterred by his unenthusiastic reception in Portugal, Columbus then sought support for his venture from the Spanish rulers, Ferdinand and Isabella. After many months of waiting, he finally managed to convince Isabella of the feasibility of finding a direct route to the Indies. And so, with the title 'Admiral of the Ocean Sea', and carrying a Latin passport, which stated 'By these presents we dispatch the noble man Christopher Columbus with three Equipped caravels over the Ocean Sea toward the region of India for certain reasons and purposes', Columbus finally sailed from Palos, southern Spain, on August 3, 1492.

By October 10, the crew, becoming frightened, rebelled and demanded that they turn back. Columbus persuaded them to bear with him for an additional three days.

On October 12, having traveled over 2,700 miles, a member of the near-mutinous crew sighted land. This proved to be an island in the Bahamas which Columbus claimed for

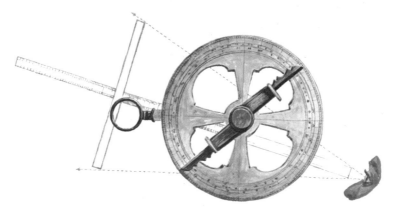

Two navigating aids—an astrolabe and a cross-staff

Spain and called San Salvador. Certain that he was near the Indies, he called the curious natives 'Indians'. He was disappointed to find no trace of gold and so taking a few natives with him as guides, he sailed on to another nearby island (Cuba). An exploration into the interior of the island failed to produce rich metals, although the Spaniards came across 'many people with a firebrand in the hand and herbs to drink the smoke thereof, as they are accustomed'. In fact, these Cuban natives smoked a primitive form of cigar which they called *tobacos*.

Undoubtedly the expedition proved disappointing to the Spaniards who failed to find the spices and rich metals that Columbus had convinced them would be plentiful in the

Columbus' three ships, the Niña, Pinta and Santa María

Flamingos

Orient. Nevertheless, among the exhibits taken back to Spain were corn, cassava, native cotton and—to be immediately adopted by the sailors—a hammock. Although the Spaniards were unable to extract information on the sources from the natives, they noticed that many of the Indians wore bangles and necklaces at least partially made of gold. It was this fact rather than a wish to convert the 'Indians' that attracted some of the Spaniards who agreed to stay behind in a garrison on the island of San Domingo.

Columbus finally sailed back to Spain in January 1493 to an enthusiastic reception. Ferdinand and Isabella welcomed him as a hero and readily agreed to finance a second voyage. The object of this second expedition was theoretically to colonize the island of Hispaniola (now divided into Haiti and

An Alligator

the Dominican Republic). In fact, Columbus' success would be measured in terms of the gold he could bring back. In this respect all his further voyages must be termed dismal failures. 'It was June 1496 before he found himself again in the harbor of Cadiz. People had crowded down to greet the great discoverer, but instead of a joyous crew, flushed with new success and rich with the spoils of the golden Indies, a feeble train of wretched men crawled ashore—thin, miserable, and ill . . . (Columbus) was utterly broken down with

Columbus lands on Hispaniola December 5, 1492

all he had been through.'

Before he died, discredited and alone, Columbus prophesied his place in history: 'By the Divine Will I have placed under the sovereignty of the King and Queen an Other World, whereby Spain which was reckoned poor, is to become the richest of all countries.' Ironically, nearly 500 years later it is not Spain but a large part of that 'Other World' that has become 'the richest of all countries'.

13

The Western Route

Columbus made so mild an impression on his own age that Benvenuto Cellini, one of its most celebrated men, never mentioned him or his voyages in his *Memoirs*.

Nevertheless Columbus' journeys were to stimulate three other countries—France, England and the Netherlands—into acquiring colonial possessions of their own. This muscling into the Spanish Empire continued until both England and France had firmly established themselves in North America.

Initially the prime object was still to get to the East. This motive spurred on several voyages of discovery after Columbus' epic find. At first, England approached the new lands timidly. She was a poor country surrounded by enemies; Scotland in the north; Ireland in the west and, strongest of all, France in the east. And although she gradually grew stronger every year, the English monarchs of the house of Tudor were cautious and watchful.

John Cabot, a skilled navigator, was an Italian who eventually came to England and settled in Bristol, a southwest coastal port, particularly favorable for explorers of the New World. Although it is unlikely that he was influenced by Columbus' voyages, Cabot also believed that the East might be more easily reached by sailing west. On March 5, 1496 he was granted a patent by King Henry VII to 'sail to the east, west, or north, with five ships carrying the English flag, to seek and discover all the islands, countries, regions, or provinces of pagans in whatever part of the world'. Henry was to receive one-fifth of the profits, and Cabot was to avoid any direct confrontation with the Spanish. Very little is known of the actual journey except a brief contemporary account which states: 'In the year 1497 John Cabot, a Venetian, and his son Sebastian discovered on the 24th of June, about five in the morning, that land to which no person had before ventured to sail, which they named Prima Vista or first seen, because, as I believe, it was the first part seen by them from the sea. The inhabitants use the skins and furs of wild beasts for garments, which they hold in as high estimation as we do our finest clothes. The soil yields no useful production, but it abounds in white bears and deer much larger

John Cabot embarked on his voyages from Bristol, England.

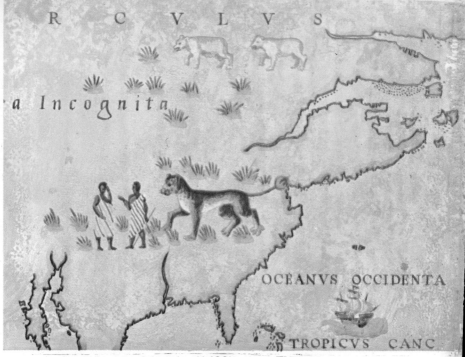

An early map of America (1499)

than ours. Its coast produces vast quantities of large fish—great seals, salmons, soles about a yard in length, and prodigious quantities of cod.'

Cabot was greatly acclaimed on his return to England and Henry VII gave him a £10 reward. However, his later explorations proved disappointing, and the teeming fisheries he had discovered off Newfoundland were soon to be exploited by the French and Portuguese.

Years later, Cabot's reports and charts of his voyages along the North American coast would be used as the legal basis for England's claim to most of the North American continent. But in Cabot's time a voyage that brought back no immediate wealth was rated a failure, and so for several years England drew back into herself. It was not until 50 years later, when Queen Elizabeth I lent her support to New World explorers, did England once again participate in discovery.

In the meantime both the Spanish and Portuguese were slowly opening up unknown routes; Vasco da Gama gave Portugal a sea route to the Orient. Pedro Alvares Cabral landed in a bay in Brazil in 1500, taking possession of that country for Portugal. From Spain sailed men who had served under Columbus, including a Florentine merchant, Amerigo Vespucci. On his return from his voyage of 1499, he wrote a somewhat exaggerated account of his finds in what was at last accepted as a new continent, and not Asia. 'It is proper to call it a New World,' Vespucci wrote. 'Men of old said over and over again that there was no land south of the Equator. But this last voyage of mine has proved them wrong, since in southern regions I have found a country more thickly inhabited by people and animals than our Europe or Asia or Africa.' The account was widely read. As a result, in 1507 a German cartographer, Martin Waldseemüller, suggested that the lands should be called *America*. The suggestion was readily accepted as it was clear that Vespucci had discovered a new continent: 'wherefore the new continent ought to be called America from its discoverer Amerigo, a man of rare ability, inasmuch as Europe and Asia derived their name from women.'

Amerigo Vespucci and a map of his voyages

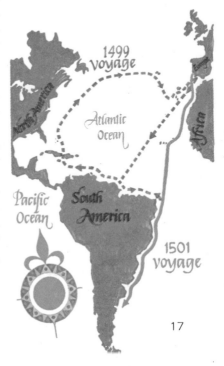

17

At that period of history the Pope in Rome was still the 'king of kings', and in 1494 he had proclaimed through a Papal Bull that Spain and Portugal could take and divide the heathen lands of the new continent between them. However, this arrangement could not avert the hungry looks of the other European countries.

Even so, for the next 50 years Portugal built up a vast empire in the East under such men as Albuquerque and Almeida; an empire bursting with riches far greater than any that had yet been found across the Atlantic Ocean. Portugal's lack of interest in the Western Hemisphere allowed Spain to explore north and south of the area Columbus had visited, unchecked by her age-old rival.

In 1508 Alonso de Ojeda began Spanish settlement of the American mainland at Panama. Five years later 'a man of action rather than judgment', Vasco Nûñez de Balboa, marched across Panama's 45-mile isthmus and became the first man to sight the Pacific from the West.

Between 1519 and 1522, Ferdinand Magellan—a Portuguese in the employ of Spain—worked his way down the South American coast, rounded the tip through the strait which now bears his name, and entered the Pacific, completing the first circumnavigation of the globe.

In both 1524 and 1525, another Portuguese in the service of Spain, Estevan Gomes, made a thorough survey of the east coast of North America from Newfoundland to Florida. This survey proved to be immensely useful to later explorers, though Gomes' hopes—'To see whether among the multitudes of windings and the vast diversities of our ocean any passage can be found leading to the Kingdom of him we commonly call the Grand Khan'—were doomed to failure.

There were several other celebrated Spanish expeditions, to the New World, but Spain was not the only devoutly Catholic country interested in the new lands. France had just come to the conclusion that the Pope's decision, giving half the world to Spain and half to Portugal, should be ignored. The matter had been unimportant when nothing of interest or value seemed to exist on the far side of the Atlantic Ocean: France had been able to work up very little

Pope Alexander VI and the Papal Bull of 1494

Jacques Cartier discovered the St. Lawrence River

enthusiasm for the exploits of Columbus, and still less for those of John Cabot. But now things were placed in a different perspective.

François I of France (1515–47) not only ignored the Pope, he more practically sent a Florentine sailor, Giovanni da Verrazano, across the Atlantic to join the search for a northwest passage to Asia. Verrazano discovered the Hudson River. A few years later François sent a French seaman, Jacques Cartier, on the same quest.

From the moment Cartier set sail in 1534 from St. Malo with two small ships and 60 men, Spain had a rival.

Cartier made two important voyages and in each of them explored the mysterious St. Lawrence River. The French sailed up as far as they could hoping that this was the long-sought northwest passage. Cartier described the bay still called Chaleur Bay: 'We named this the Warm Bay, for the country is warmer even than Spain and exceedingly pleasant.' He named the southern point Hope Cape, but then he reached rapids and was discouraged; though at the far side, it still seemed possible that he had entered a strait.

Keeping to a northerly course, Cartier eventually anchored at what is now Gaspé Bay. Cartier records that here, 'on the 24th July, we made a great cross thirty feet high, on which we hung up a shield with three fleur-de-lis, and inscribed the cross with this motto: *"Vive le roi de France."* When this was finished, in the presence of all the natives, we all knelt down before the cross, holding up our hands to heaven and praising God.' In May 1535, Cartier was commissioned to continue his exploration of these new lands. Reaching a 'very fine and large bay, full of islands, and with channels of entrance and exit in all winds' on the Labrador Coast, Cartier named it 'Baye Saint Laurens', because he discovered it on the feast of St. Lawrence.

Indians told Cartier that he was approaching the mouth of a great river (now the St. Lawrence) which narrowed 'as we approach Canada, where the water is fresh!' (Canada was an Indian word meaning a town or village.)

Although he explored further inland, Cartier's expedition was soon caught by the

An 'esquimau'—Eskimo

bitter Canadian winter, and it was May 1536 before he was able to sail for home.

France could now lay claim to a vast new country, though the erroneous theory that the St. Lawrence was the gateway to the East persisted among French explorers for many years. When the French came to Lake St. Louis, with its great size, and vast area of shimmering water, they were convinced they had come to the Pacific. *'La Chine!'* they shouted, pointing west. However, the new land eventually became known by the name 'Canada', given it by the Huron and Iroquois Indians who lived there. Jacques Cartier liked the name and retained it.

French explorers joined their compatriot Cartier in investigating the northern parts of the American continent. They visited Labrador, Newfoundland and all the places the Vikings had seen more than 500 years before. But their investigation was more thorough, and tales came back, well authenticated, of many different Indian tribes, including some, far north, who called themselves something like *'Esquimaux'* (Eskimo) and dressed entirely in skins.

By these explorations France had acquired—at least in her own eyes—some right to a large northern section of America. Spain by that time was far too engrossed in her lands further south to pay much attention to the French in the frozen north. She had already discovered, in Central and South America, riches of unparalleled magnificence—gold, silver and precious jewels. It seemed to the Spanish that there was little, if any, riches to be gained in the north. Thus the two great Catholic powers avoided conflict over their new territories.

To the Spaniards, the American natives they met—a very different sort of Indian to those in the north—were beings to be exploited and used. Aztecs and Incas only existed as a means to an end (though the majority of the Spaniards tried to force the Christian religion on the peoples they conquered). To the French, perhaps because there was at first very little worth plundering, the Indians were fascinating and very human individuals. Frenchmen learned one or more of their various languages, studied their customs and befriended them from the outset. It was a policy which was soon to pay dividends.

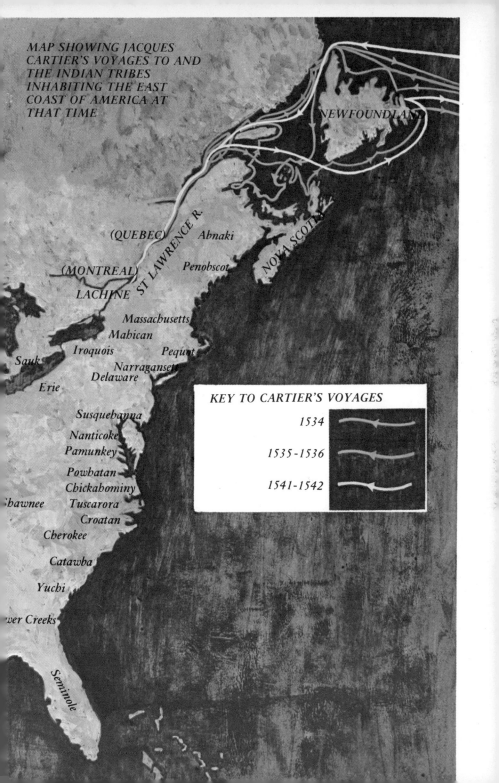

MAP SHOWING JACQUES
CARTIER'S VOYAGES TO AND
THE INDIAN TRIBES
INHABITING THE EAST
COAST OF AMERICA AT
THAT TIME

NEWFOUNDLAND

(QUEBEC)   Abnaki

(MONTREAL)   Penobscot

LACHINE   ST LAWRENCE R.

NOVA SCOTIA

Massachusetts
Mahican
Iroquois   Pequot
Sauk   Narraganset
Delaware
Erie

Susquehanna
Nanticoke
Pamunkey
Powhatan
Chickahominy
Shawnee   Tuscarora
Croatan
Cherokee

Catawba

Yuchi

ver Creeks

Seminole

KEY TO CARTIER'S VOYAGES

1534

1535-1536

1541-1542

The Spanish Seaborne Empire

It was 1513 when Balboa first sighted the Pacific Ocean after hacking his way through the 45-mile-wide Isthmus of Panama. In the same year his compatriot, Juan Ponce de León, also achieved something of considerable importance. Immensely brave and incorrigibly greedy, Ponce de León was typical of his age. The seas around the Americas in the sixteenth century were full of Spanish ships. There were literally dozens of Spaniards whose contributions to ultimate discovery of America were extremely significant.

Juan Ponce de León discovered, explored and named Florida in 1513. In fact, whether he knew it or not, he was leading the first Spanish expedition to the North American continent. By then he was an elderly man, and the reasons for his journey were strange. Years before, he had sailed with Columbus and more recently he had discovered Puerto Rico. In 1513, he had heard stories of an extraordinary fountain on a magic island which the natives called 'Rimini'.

In fact it was not an island, and it had no fountain. It was inhabited by Cherokee Indians who—on this occasion— seemed friendly enough. After naming it 'Land of Flowers' and formally taking possession of it for his king and queen, a disappointed Ponce de León sailed away.

On a second trip, eight years later, Ponce de León rounded the tip of Florida, giving his name to a bay on its west coast. This time he found that the Indians were no longer friendly, and he was fatally wounded. He was never to know that the site of his earlier North American landing would become the first permanent settlement on that continent—the Spanish fort of St. Augustine.

In the meantime, the Spaniards had wasted no time in organizing their first discovery, the West Indies, and adventurers poured out from Spain to make their fortunes. One of these was Hernando Cortez—'a respectable gentleman of good birth'—who had failed to get a legal degree at Salamanca·University and was sent out to Hispaniola by

Ponce de León is attacked by Indians in Florida

his father. Cortez was only 19 years old when he arrived there in 1504, but he was immediately given a large tract of land and natives to work it. Seven years later he was given the opportunity of joining the Velázquez expedition which was sailing off to conquer a large neighboring island.

This presented no problems: the people of Cuba fled in terror, and within weeks the island was in the firm grip of a Spanish administration. Hernando Cortez prospered greatly from this trip, and he later was appointed magistrate of the chief town, Santo Domingo.

It was shortly after Cortez's rise that the full import of the discovery of Mexico became clear to every Spaniard in Cuba. An expedition had left the island in February 1517, 'steering toward the setting sun' in the hope of new discoveries, and from a landfall in Yucatan, they had explored inland. There they discovered the interesting fact that the Mayan people, unlike any others they had encountered in the Western Hemisphere, made houses of stone. They did not realize that these people were also highly skilled mathematicians and astronomers. The Mayans were also ferocious fighters, managing to drive the Spaniards back into the sea, across which they retreated to Cuba.

Velázquez sent a better-armed expedition the following year which brought back gold, as well as one or two disquieting tales: at one place they had come across the bodies of two young boys. Near them, on an altar in a golden bowl, were their still-warm hearts.

To Velazquez, and to those close to him like Cortez, only the gold mattered. But the fact that the Indians were reported to indulge in some sort of human sacrifice also gave the Spaniards the moral reason for conquering them in the cause of Christianity, although the main object of any further expedition was to bring back gold.

Cortez talked Velázquez into putting him in charge of the expedition. But even before the expedition sailed from Havana, on February 10, 1519, Velázquez had begun to regret it. With a blinding flash of intuition he realized that this unscrupulous young adventurer intended to carve out an

Cortez lands in Mexico—he was eventually to destroy the Aztec empire and to loot its treasury.

el Grande Templo de Mexico

Above: Temple of Tenochtitlan

Left: Three forms of human sacrifice—from an Aztec Codex
—and an Obsidian sacrificial knife

empire for himself—not for Diego de Velázquez.

Velázquez was right—but it was too late. Eleven vessels
had slipped out of Havana harbor and the 653 men on board
would—incredibly—seize Mexico. Cortez was resolved to
say nothing to the Indians about Cuba or Velázquez. As far
as they were concerned, he had come all the way from Spain,
an emissary of her king, bringing that king's protection and
with it the priceless knowledge of a god. In exchange for all
this the Mexicans would hand over riches which Cortez
would divide between himself and his king. And the king
would make Cortez governor of the new domain.

Cortez was often fantastically lucky, but he was also a
brave and remarkable man. One of those who accompanied
him was Bernal Diaz who later wrote an account of the
expedition entitled *Conquest of New Spain*. Diaz described
Cortez as 'a tall man, well proportioned and robust, whose
face had little color and was inclined to be grayish, whose

hair and beard were black and thin. He had courage, spirit, and was an extremely skillful horseman and swordsman. Cortez was also a Latin scholar and something of a poet. Each morning he recited prayers and heard Mass with devoutness.'

In a mood of great enthusiasm the expedition sailed to the north of the Yucatan peninsula, past the land of the Mayans, heading west to the coast from where the previous expedition had brought back gold and strange tales. Inland from it lived the Aztecs, far richer than the Mayans, the Tabascoans and the other tribes.

Cortez landed all his force where the city of Vera Cruz now stands (it was destined to become the commercial capital of New Spain). He was immediately attacked, but his superior strategy—and the terrifying, supernatural-seeming horses he had brought to a land where all beasts of burden were unknown—won the day. So humbled were the warriors of Tabasco that they willingly accepted the King of Spain as their overlord and eagerly embraced Christianity (if only for

NORTH AMERICA

ATLANTIC OCEAN

MEXICO

PACIFIC OCEAN

CARIBBEAN SEA

the present.) They presented Cortez with some 20 young women as a gift. He distributed them among his captains, later retaining one of the most personable for himself. Dona Marina, as he christened her, was to play a considerable part in the Spanish conquest of Mexico, for she turned out to be of Aztec descent, speaking that language as well as Tabascoan and Mayan. As at least one Spaniard with the expedition spoke Mayan, Dona Marina provided the all-important means of communicating with the Aztecs.

The Spaniards set sail again. The episode had been distinctly profitable, but for a reason far more strange and subtle than the *conquistadores* can have surmised. They did not anchor off the Mexican coast until the eve of Good Friday; and this chance happening sealed the fate of the Aztec empire and its tragic ruler, Montezuma.

Many years before the Aztecs had exiled their great god, Quetzalcoatl. To be more precise, the Aztecs had allowed another stronger god, Tezcatlipoca, to do it. Tezcatlipoca was a fearsome god who demanded human sacrifice on an enormous scale if he were to keep the sun alight and the corn crop growing. Quetzalcoatl had preached against

Left: an early map of
Mexico City

Right: the god
Quetzalcoatl

31

human sacrifice and the ritual tearing out of hearts from live victims, but his people would not listen. As he embarked on a magic raft, heading over the eastern horizon into exile, Quetzalcoatl had said, 'I will return on a Nine Wind Day of a One Reed Year, and re-establish my rule. It will be a time of tribulation.'

Incredibly, according to the astrological Aztec calendar, with its 52-year cycle, the last 'One Reed Year' had been 1467 and all Mexico had shivered in anticipation of Quetzalcoatl's vengeful return. He had not returned. It was now 1519—another One Reed Year. Good Friday in the Christian calendar chanced, that year, to be a Nine Wind Day, the day on which a white-skinned, black-bearded god, dressed in black arrived by sea from the east.

Because it was Good Friday, the devout Cortez was dressed entirely in black. As he landed on the coast of Mexico, the news was carried inland, up into the mountains, and Montezuma believed that Quetzalcoatl had returned.

Montezuma was terrified, but he rushed a team of emissaries to the coast. They brought turkeys, dogs, and a very fat slave, Cuitlapitoc, whom the others were to sacrifice if the god should want to eat him or drink his blood. The fact that the puzzled and slightly horrified Cortez refused the delicacy was proof, if any were needed, that this was indeed Quetzalcoatl.

Cortez and his small army then made their way slowly up-country, while Montezuma sent daily messengers from his great palace in Tenochtitlan, the beautiful stone city built on an island. It was situated on a lake which has since dried up. Each messenger bore gold, silver and precious jewels, and each urged the 'god' not to tire himself with the journey, but to accept these gifts and return peacefully across the sea from where he had come. With the treasure came the little dogs, the 'chihuahuas' that the Aztecs bred for the table, together with turkeys and other delicacies. Cortez thanked the Emperor Montezuma for each gift, but he continued to advance.

It was three hard months before the Spaniards reached their goal. As they approached the causeways, over five miles long, which led to Tenochtitlan (now rebuilt as

Mexico City) one of the party wrote that: 'Many of us were disposed to doubt the reality of the scene before us and to suspect we were in a dream. I thought we had been transported by magic to the terrestrial paradise.'

At any moment as they entered the city the Spanish army could have been annihilated by the overwhelming numbers of Indians. But instead they conquered a vast country and an advanced civilization because its emperor thought their leader was a god. Not all the Aztec nobles agreed with Montezuma (he was accidentally killed by one of his people), but it was too late: a 'god' had control of their destiny. Cortez did not have it all his own way. With the death of Montezuma who had believed in his divinity, he found he had to fight others who did not. But Cortez eventually won, and by 1521 Aztec Mexico was a part of Spain, with Hernando Cortez as its self-proclaimed viceroy.

A decade later another Spaniard, Francisco Pizarro, discovered the fabulous silver mines of Peru.

By now all Europe was aware of the wealth of the New World, including the

Turkeys

Chihuahuas

Snakes

Corn

33

English. Her sailors started to attack Spanish ships on the high seas and seize their cargo. This seemed an easy way of getting a share of the New World's treasure.

The Spaniards pressed on in search of more treasure. Seven years after Cortez's subjugation of Mexico, the first sizeable expedition dropped anchor off the coast of North America. Pánfilo de Narváez and 300 men prepared to disembark at what is now the city of Tampa on the west coast of Florida. Following Cortez's example, Narváez had brought horses as well—though far more than Cortez had thought advisable—'to strike terror into the hearts of the inhabitants'—but they did nothing of the sort. The expedition became a nightmare from which only three Spaniards and one Negro slave escaped, and these only because a storm wrecked their ship before they reached the shore. Most of the other Spaniards were butchered by the same west Florida Indians who had killed Ponce de León, the rest being taken into slavery.

The leader of the shipwrecked survivors was Cabeza de Vaca, and the winds which sent him and his three companions drifting across the Gulf of Mexico deposited them eventually on the coast of Texas. From here they worked their way overland along the northern edge of Mexico and into California, where like Balboa, but after considerably more difficulty with the Indians, they sighted the Pacific. Cabeza de Vaca eventually got back to Spain, and by embellishing his accounts he gave a sudden new impetus to Spanish exploration.

One of those now impelled to explore was Hernando De Soto, already wealthy from his earlier travels in Peru with Pizarro, who set off from Florida, on foot, in search of 'El Dorado', 'The Golden Land'. It was Columbus who had brought back, among his tales of fine buildings and tall steeples, the legend of this land of fantastic riches. So wealthy was De Soto that though Spain's ruler (now the Emperor Charles V) gave his blessing to the 'El Dorado' search, he insisted that it be carried out at De Soto's expense. So in 1539 the intrepid explorer set off with a few mounted companions from the same west coast of Florida that had cost the lives of so many of his compatriots.

The routes of Narváez and Cabeza de Vaca

It was a fantastic journey, through unknown, unexplored and largely hostile territory, lasting three years. In 1541 De Soto reached the Mississippi River near Memphis. It must have been a thrilling and unnerving sight, even if De Soto was not aware that he had stumbled upon the longest river in the world, some 4,800 miles long, from its source to the Gulf of Mexico.

But it was not 'El Dorado'. The Spanish party crossed the river to the future Fort Smith, Arkansas, and spent the winter there. Continuing their search they had several skirmishes with the Indians, and eventually De Soto, weak from wounds and fever, came back to the river he had found. There he died, and his surviving companions struggled to safety in Mexico after an absence of more than four years.

During these years, another Spaniard, Francisco Vásquez de Coronado, explored northward from Mexico. He too was in search of gold, a gold as mythical as De Soto's 'El Dorado', and he too set forth on horseback. He explored west Texas, Colorado and New Mexico during the years 1541 and 1542, before he eventually despaired of finding treasure on 'this limitless plain'.

His actual discoveries meant very little to Coronado: he was looking for treasure and the Seven Cities of Cibola, the home of the Pueblo Indians, where there would be wealth to rival that of Montezuma — or so he had been told. He found none of this but, unlike De Soto, he survived his wanderings and brought back a great deal of information about the southwest and its indigenous people, the Navajo and the Pueblo Indians.

He also saw, without knowing what they were, the remains of prehistoric villages, the homes of the men and their descendants, who had crossed the Bering Strait 20,000 years before. These remains are still there today, a joy to archeologists proving that this part of the North American continent must have been far more hospitable than it is now.

De Soto sights the Mississippi River

While Coronado was moving north and west with his party of horsemen, Hernando de Alarcón set sail from Acapulco on the Pacific coast of Mexico, in order to 'support' him and if possible join up with his party. Considering the unfamiliarity of the coast, the vast unknown area inland and the primitive methods of survey, it seems incredible now that he could have entertained the thought of winning through to his gold-maddened compatriot.

But anything was possible in and around this new Spanish empire. Unbelievable treasure had already been found and much of it shipped back to old Spain (whose economy would, perversely, founder in a few years from the surfeit); there were greater treasures yet unfound; and the people and the astonishing birds and beasts and fishes of America made this a magic land where anything seemed possible.

A Pueblo Indian settlement

Alarcón came remarkably close to a rendezvous with Coronado, but the debt we owe him is for the important discovery that the part of America that was to become California is not an island, but a peninsula. Many sailors—not all of them Spanish—had sailed along California's eastern and western coasts, satisfying themselves that this long thin pencil off the west coast of Mexico was an island. Alarcón explored what is now called the Gulf of California and was fascinated by the weird fishes contained in its waters, such as the flying fish which he had seen before, and the ferocious barracuda, which he had not.

At the top of the gulf Alarcón boldly sailed into the Colorado River and pressed on northward as it narrowed, and its banks grew from sandy slopes to steep hills, to sheer red cliffs. He realized—somehow—that the extraordinary river he was ascending was the same one Coronado had come to, only much further upstream. Optimistically, he buried some letters for Coronado's party before turning about and sailing back to sea.

Alarcón's view of the Colorado was mysterious and awe-inspiring. The view Coronado had was very different.

He had been traveling for months across the baking plains of the southwest. Often his party had been perilously short of water and hungry for want of food. Moreover, the Indian tribes they met were not wealthy at all.

One of Coronado's lieutenants, Pedro de Tovar, was sent ahead of the main party, and he visited Hopi Indian vil-

Spanish ships in the Colorado River

lages in northern Arizona; another lieutenant, Garcîa Lopéz de Cárdenas, discovered the Grand Canyon. Yet another, Hernando de Alvarado, visited Acoma and the Pueblos of the Pecos and the Rio Grande.

The Grand Canyon, one of the great natural wonders of the world, is a foot or two deeper now than it was when the Spaniards first saw it, for the river eats into it steadily. But with a depth of between 4,000 and 7,000 feet, it is safe to assume that it looks today very much like it looked then. The Grand Canyon is in fact a stretch of river, in

Flying Fish

what is now Arizona, approximately 217 miles in length, with a width, from rim to rim, of between 4 and 18 miles.

Meanwhile Coronado had been told by Indians of the Turk tribe that there existed a wealthy city in the east called Quivara. In this city a rich ruler 'took his afternoon nap under a great tree on which were hung a great number of little gold bells, which put him to sleep as they swung in the air . . . Everyone had their ordinary dishes made of wrought plate, and the jugs and bowls were of gold.' As soon as they could organize themselves the Spaniards set off again, taking with them the Indian slave, who had told them of the city of Quivara. Of the country they passed through, one of them wrote: 'the country is like a bowl, so that when a man sits down, the horizon surrounds him all around at the distance of a musket shot.'

Quivara, which they reached after a northward journey of 42 days, proved to be a terrible disappointment. The

Barracuda

Grand Canyon in Arizona

marvelous city was in fact a group of grass huts belonging to the Wichita Indians on the Kansas River.

One of the party summed up the expedition's feelings when he complained that 'they had seen nothing but cows (buffalos) and sky'.

And so, virtually at the sixteenth century's halfway mark, one comes—more or less—to the end of important Spanish exploration in the New World. When the Spaniards come into the narrative again it is not as explorers; for the time had come for other nations to consider settling in this new land. Even the English, who watched from a distance the explorations of more ambitious and powerful nations, would soon be sailing westward, bringing seeds to sow and tools for building.

An appropriate way to end the Spaniards part in the discovery of North America is to quote the words of a Portuguese navigator, Juan Rodriguez Cabrillo, who discovered the bay of San Diego on the California coast in 1542, two years after Alarcón's trip up the Colorado. It was, and is, a wonderful harbor, some fifteen miles from the Mexican border. Already, inland of it, there were Spaniards:

'Having cast anchor in the bay, we went ashore where there were Indians. Three of these waited, but all the rest fled. To these three we gave some presents, and they said by signs that in the interior men like the Spaniards had passed. They gave signs of great fear.

On the night of this day the sailors went ashore to fish; and it appears that here there were some Indians and that

they began to shoot at them with arrows and wounded three sailors.

Next day we went further into the port and brought back two small boys, who understood nothing by signs. We gave shirts to both and sent them away immediately.

Next day three adult Indians came to the ships and said by signs that in the interior men like us were traveling about. They made signs that they were killing many Indians and that they were afraid.

These people are comely and large. They wear skins of animals.'

The first French settlement in Florida

Early French Exploration and Settlement

Like England, France had not attempted to colonize America for more than 50 years after the Spanish and Portuguese had laid the foundations of their empires. As already noted, Jacques Cartier had searched for the northwest passage, discovering instead the great St. Lawrence River. A few years later, in 1541, another Frenchman, Jean François de La Roque, Sieur de Roberval, laid plans for a settlement on the St. Lawrence. Roberval, still thinking of the river as a means of reaching the East, envisaged his settlement being a strategic stop on the route. In this venture he enlisted the help of Cartier, who agreed to go ahead and commence construction of the settlement. But as with his early journeys, Cartier once again found the cold of a Canadian winter unbearable and he decided to abandon the project and return to France. On his return journey he met Roberval going the other way, who ordered Cartier to carry out his part of the arrangement. But Cartier was sick of the freezing cold and his ships sailed back to France, ignoring his leader's orders. Roberval in his turn tried to cope with

Jean Ribaut

the climate but was forced to go back, having barely survived the winter of 1542–43.

Although this disastrous attempt at settlement did not entirely discourage France's interest in North America, it did tend to make them think of settling in another part of America where there was a more equable climate and living conditions.

It was in 1513 that Ponce de León had landed, high up on the east coast of Florida, looking in vain for his Fountain of Youth. It was left to the French, half a century later, to start a colony on the site.

There was another factor which had as great an influence on the discovery of North America as a greed for gold: religious persecution. The first to flee from it were the Protestants of France, styling themselves 'Huguenots'. The first party of Protestants (Huguenots) sailed under the command of Nicholas Durand de Villegagnon in 1555: a venture supported by both John Calvin, the religious reformer, and Gaspard de Coligny, the French Protestant leader. The French party landed on an island off the coast of Brazil. Unfortunately, the would-be colonists had a falling out among them-

The building of Fort Caroline

selves, and this factor, coupled with active hostility from the Portuguese conquerors of Brazil, ruined any chance of success.

In 1562 another French Protestant expedition left for the New World, led this time by Jean Ribaut of Dieppe. They arrived during the summer amidst an unfamiliar and blistering heat at the River of May (St. John's River) in the Spanish territory of Florida. But the party of 30 were unprepared for what they found—in particular, the unfriendly and treacherous Indians. They also failed—like so many early colonists in America—to grow or hunt food for themselves, preferring to spend their days looking for gold. As a result when they tried to return to France the party nearly starved—actually drawing lots as to who should be eaten first by his comrades. A final disaster befell them when, in sight of French soil, they were captured by an English ship.

Two years later another Frenchman, René de Laudonnière landed boldly in much the same place, with another band of Huguenots. There was nothing to show that an earlier group had settled there, and after some consideration of this

and a study of the coastline, Laudonnière moved on to
the St. John's River, still in Florida, and made his own
settlement.

The Huguenots called the spot Fort Caroline (after Charles
IX). Were it not for Spanish jealousy that spot would today
be the site of America's first permanent settlement. Laudonnière and his tough settlers made a better job of getting on
with their Indian neighbors than had their predecessors and
Fort Caroline grew rapidly. But the Spanish king grew angry:
Spain had explored the entire southeastern coast, and he
was determined to have the land remain part of Spain.

Even worse from the Spanish point of view, these particular Frenchmen, flouting the Pope's edict that all this land
was Spanish, were infidels, not Catholics. The Spanish king
was now Philip II, and he rushed an expedition out to the
New World territory to deal with them. In the expedition
were a number of priests, dedicated men, with no interest in
gold or other treasure. From now on, these men would form
an important part of every Spanish expedition, and it would
be largely due to their efforts that Spain was able to hold
onto much of the land she had entered to exploit.

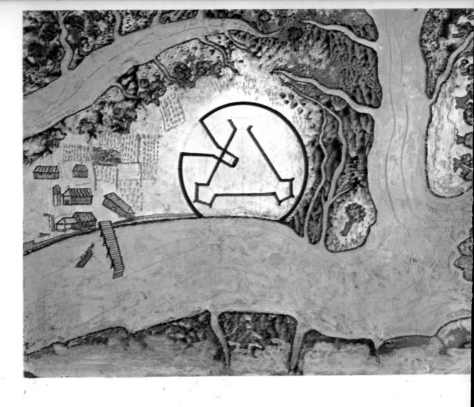

The earliest map of Fort St. Augustine

The year was 1565—and the Spaniards, anxious to teach the French a lesson, chose to land on the exact spot where Ponce de León had disembarked to look for his Fountain of Youth. Largely as a result of the civilizing influence of the priests who traveled with the expedition, this spot (the Indians called it 'Seloy') would become the first permanent settlement in America.

The expedition landed on the calendar day dedicated to Saint Augustine, and that immediately became the colony's name. The chaplain of the expedition kept a diary from which we can take this description of the landing:

Carrying a cross, I proceeded at the head of our column, singing the hymn Te Deum Laudamus. Our General marched straight to where I halted and, kneeling, kissed the cross. A large number of Indians looked upon these ceremonies and imitated whatever they saw done. Thereupon the General took possession of the country in the name of his Majesty.

All the officers then took an oath of allegiance to him as their General and the overlord of the whole country.'

'Overlord of the whole country'. Small chance then for Fort Caroline, struggling to survive further along the coast. By this time Fort Caroline was in fairly desperate straits, and it was only through the timely appearance of the English privateer, John Hawkins, in August 1565 that the settlement was able to survive. Hawkins sold Laudonnière food and one of his ships, and soon after Ribaut arrived with supplies and reinforcements from France. It was at this juncture that the Spaniards appeared on the scene. One wrote frantically: 'they put the Indies in a Crucible, for we are compelled to pass in front of their port, and with the greatest ease they can sally out with their armadas to seek us, and easily return home when it suits them.'

Philip II then instructed Don Pedro Menéndez de Avilés to drive the French out of Florida 'by what means you see fit' and to build a Spanish colony that would prevent future French settlement.

Ribaut, having avoided a fight with the Spanish at the mouth of St. John's followed their fleet to St. Augustine.

Fort St. Augustine as it is today

This was a fatal mistake, for Fort Caroline was now virtually defenseless and Menéndez de Avilés marched overland with the Spanish troops and wiped out the colony, killing most of the French. One of the few to survive the massacre was Laudonnière, who finally got back to France in 1566. His account of this, the first colony in North America, was published in 1586 entitled *Histoire notable de la Floride*. Meantime, Ribaut, in his turn, had been murdered by the Spanish when he and his followers had been shipwrecked in a storm south of St. Augustine.

This action brought to an abrupt end French aspirations in Florida. Indeed there was virtually no French exploration in America for more than ten years mainly because France was being torn apart at that time by religious and dynastic conflicts.

Then in 1578 the Marquis de la Roche was commissioned to colonize the area explored by Jacques Cartier over 40 years before. Even though the first expedition setting out in 1584 was wrecked, the French were not deterred. In 1598, 60 people were landed on Sable Island, while the ship they

The massacre of the French at Fort Caroline

had sailed in went on to explore the coastline. The ship was unable to return due to the appalling weather conditions in the area, and the wretched French settlers left on Sable Island were forced to stay there for five years before they were rescued by a special expedition.

In the same year that the party was rescued—1603—the Commander de Chastes was given monopoly of the fur trade by the French king. De Chastes went into partnership with the merchants of St. Malo and Rouen, sending an expedition out under the leadership of Dupont Gravé and Samuel de Champlain. The result was the establishment in 1604 of the first successful French colony at Port Royal in Acadia, the present-day maritime province of Canada. Four years later Champlain was to found the great city of Quebec.

For more than a century and a half the French had vainly tried to establish a claim in the New World. Paradoxically they proved most successful at a disastrous period in French history when the Protestant revolt in Catholic France had divided the country into two armed camps bent on destroying each other. But the mounting persecution of the French Huguenots was to drive countless of their number to America

where they contributed enormously to the founding of the European colonies in North America.

At this stage it would be beneficial to look briefly at the natives, the 'Indians' with whom the white men had to share the American continent for the next 300 years.

The Indians conquered by the Spaniards in the southwest area of the future United States were 'pueblo-builders', that is nonmigratory, agricultural people.

However, the other European countries who 'invaded' the eastern seaboard of the continent, found that these regions were peopled by tribes of Woodland Indians, who were only semi-sedentary, living as much from hunting as from growing their own food.

Most of the tribes were independent, except for a few groups like the Iroquois or 'Five Nations', who joined forces in time of war.

Another group who were a great influence on the history of the eastern seaboard at this time were the Muskhogeans. This group included the

Seminole Indians

Natchez, Creeks, Choctaw, Chickasaw and Seminoles.

The relations between these Indians and the white men was divided into two periods: first, they were people to trade with for skins, and to use as guides; second, they became the enemy when the relentless westward drive of the colonists began to impinge more and more on lands previously occupied by the Indians.

Gradually the Indians were displaced either by the white men 'buying' the land or by blatant conquest. Naturally the Indians tried every means they knew, from peaceful negotiations to bloody warfare, to stop this process. But all their efforts were doomed to failure against the great Anglo-Saxon drive west. And throughout all the history of colonization that follows one must remember that all this time, balanced against the spectacular achievements of the European colonists, another civilization and culture was slowly losing its grip on the continent over which it had once ruled supreme.

Spanish soldiers

54

Elizabethan England and the New World

Queen Elizabeth I died in 1603. And one of the oddest facts in history is that, in spite of the many glories of the Elizabethan Age, when she died England did not own—or did not even claim to own—a square foot of land outside the British Isles.

However, it was during the long reign of the 'Virgin Queen'—who had already given her name to a short-lived colony—that the foundations of British rule in North America were laid. English achievement across the Atlantic may have been insignificant during the sixteenth century, but without Elizabeth's devoted support of her merchant-buccaneers and gentleman-pirates there would never have come into being the vast British Empire which began in the seventeenth century.

In a previous chapter we looked at England during the reign of King Henry VII. Henry sent John Cabot across the ocean to 'investigate the new route to the Orient', and when he returned, having landed briefly in North America, Henry gave him a £10 reward, and forgot all about Cabot's discoveries. Henry VIII ascended England's throne in 1509 and during a considerable reign marked by tyranny and over-ambitious foreign ventures he set the scene for the colonial 'boom' of the next century. His people perhaps did not realize it, but Henry VIII succeeded in making England a hard place to live in and a good place to leave. He had been excommunicated by the Pope over the problem of divorcing his first wife, and this resulted in the closing down of 616 monasteries and nunneries. These establishments sent money regularly to the Pope, and now that he had broken with Rome, Henry preferred to fill the royal coffers with this revenue.

Money did pour into the royal coffers and, much as was happening with Spain and its New World treasure, in England the riches served only to debase the coinage, making the country poorer than before. The great landowners were hard hit but quickly found a way out: they sold wool abroad and got real gold and silver in exchange.

In order to do this really profitably, they began evicting

Elizabeth I, one of England's strongest and most successful rulers their small tenants and ploughmen and raising sheep. Three shepherds took the place of 100 small farmers—and 97 hungry men set out in search of work. Henry gave active encouragement to this process. By the time Henry's daughter Elizabeth I came to the throne in 1558, the old feudal England had vanished and there was a new middle class of merchants determined to make money. Far wiser and more capable than her father, Elizabeth made it her business to help them. She stopped the minting of worthless money, encouraged agriculture, and looked around for lands with which to trade and grow rich.

Money was invested in enlarging the English navy, and seamen like Gilbert, Drake, Frobisher and countless others sailed with Elizabeth's blessing to 'trade'. This meant in effect that if they chanced upon, say, Spanish galleons laden with Mexican gold, they could interrupt their own peaceful trading voyages to board the vessel and help themselves to the contents.

Under Elizabeth a large

fleet was built up, with a heavy armament, and sent forth under men like Francis Drake and John Hawkins, ostensibly to open up trade routes. Spain was nominally at peace with England, but Drake and Hawkins knew that if they captured Spanish vessels—even in Spanish harbors—they had their queen's blessing.

Returning from one of his most celebrated voyages, Drake sailed for home via the coast of Florida and profitably raided St. Augustine where, as already noted, the Spaniards had put down the first permanent colony in North America. He reached England in triumph, and Queen Elizabeth was delighted.

Then in 1578, with five swift ships and 150 men, Drake captured a Spanish vessel carrying no less than '26 tons of silver and 80 pounds of gold', plus priceless jewels.

Left: Francis Drake

Below: sixteenth-century English ships

Walter Raleigh

This incident was one of several provocative acts which resulted in Philip II of Spain sending an 'Armada'—130 huge ships which sailed into the English Channel in July 1588 with the mission of invading an island composed of pirates and heretics.

However, the English fleet under Lord Howard of Effingham was prepared. Howard's fleet of agile well-armed, little ships—helped by violent storms—destroyed the Armada. The English themselves sustained few losses.

This was the first and last time that Spain seriously tried to invade England. All Europe soon realized that the sea battle that had just been fought in the Straits of Dover was a turning point in history. From now on English ships were the new masters of the seas. Just at a time when Spain had seemed destined to become a universal power, she had failed to consolidate her grip.

The time had come for a different stamp of man like

Walter Raleigh, whose consuming passion was to 'yet live to see it (the New World) an Inglishe nation'. The plan was for England to start to plant colonies, or companies across the vast Atlantic Ocean. These would prosper on the riches of the New World and at the same time act as revictualing posts on the never-to-be-found 'new route to the Orient'.

The collapse of the Spanish Armada was only one factor in this decision for territorial expansion. Englishmen had been sailing the world with impunity for a generation, urged on and even backed up by their queen. Not all of them had been pirates. Five years before the Armada, Sir Humphrey Gilbert had landed in Newfoundland with a royal patent from Elizabeth authorizing him to set up a colony of Englishmen under the laws of England. The colony failed, and Gilbert was drowned on the way back. But a year later, in 1584, his half-brother Sir Walter Raleigh was planning an expedition to find a site for a colony further south.

Raleigh was a soldier, not a sailor. He was also a poet,

An opossum and a raccoon

The departure of Raleigh's
second attempted colony

philosopher and courtier, and
though possessing little personal wealth, was able to
organize huge undertakings
through influence at court.
He was a favorite of Elizabeth, and with her backing he
was able to send out two ships
in March 1584, to reconnoitre
the coast immediately north
of the Spanish settlements
in Florida. The ships sailed
daringly close to those
settlements before arriving at
Roanoke Island, off what is
now North Carolina.

Early map of the 'Virginia Coast'

Finding the land to be suited for settlements, the English took possession in the name of the queen and sailed back with two Indians as exhibits. Both Raleigh and Elizabeth were delighted, and the never-to-marry queen accepted reference to her single status in the name of the new colony: it would be called 'Virginia'.

The bill that then went through the House of Commons remains the first item of American legislation in parliamentary records. On the basis of the bill, Raleigh's second colonizing expedition set sail in 1585. It comprised seven ships under Sir Richard Grenville. Sir Richard duly landed his people on Roanoke and headed home, confident that he had just planted a firm and lasting colony in the New World. He was to be disillusioned. Within a short while the colonists had turned friendly Indians into vicious enemies: the Englishmen that survived were lucky to be picked up by Francis Drake at the end of a voyage in the Caribbean, and ferried home.

England in the sixteenth century was not a tolerant country. Even the excitement of Elizabeth's reign did little to alter the persecution and poverty of many of her subjects, and there were many volunteers for a new Virginia expedition — once again backed by Raleigh — in 1587. Over 100 colonists set out, 17 of them women, 9 of them children.

The governor appointed for this colony was John White, and on August 18, 1587 the first American-born child of English parents was born in Virginia — White's granddaughter. She was named Virginia after the new colony, and White soon sailed back to England to organize supplies and settlers, leaving little Virginia Dare there with her parents and the other colonists. White did not return until 1591, delayed by the impeding war with Spain, but when he reached his colony not a trace remained. Perhaps they were massacred by Indians, perhaps they moved, perhaps they died of disease or starvation. To this day, we do not know. White and his small party were shown by the Indians a crudely carved word on a tree. It read CROATOAN, and this, they were led to believe, was the name of a nearby island. Perhaps the colonists had set off to go there. Perhaps they never had the time.

John White is remembered today for his water colors of plants and animals, and of Indian life, which are the first pictorial records that exist of American life as seen by the English.

When White left for England again, he took nothing with him, not even the 'tobacco' which earlier visitors had brought back, or the strange 'opossum' and 'raccoon' skins and the brightly colored feathers of weird birds.

In any case, the weed that the Indians called 'tobacco' was of little interest to Europeans. The Indians smoked it in long pipes, but the taste was harsh and few white men liked it. Years would go by before a way of 'curing' tobacco was invented by John Rolfe, a Virginia planter, so that it was pleasant to smoke. When that happened, 'Virginia' would become

The sole relic of the first Virginia colony

Francis Drake's ship, the *Golden Hind*

self-sufficient and eventually wealthy. But it would be a new Virginia, trying to erase the memory of the old.

In 1589, it seemed unlikely that there ever would be a Virginia in the New World. The great victory over the Armada had made colonization that much simpler, by eliminating Spanish forces. But England, understandably, paused, aware of the hazards of settling new lands.

In fact, 18 years were to go by before the next party sailed. By then, England had a new ruler, vain and often foolish James I, who, nevertheless, succeeded in planting thriving colonies where other colonies had failed. He made pronouncements like 'I shall made them conform, or I will harry them out of the land, or else do worse'. And the little pockets of Englishmen and women forced to emigrate since the days of Henry VIII suddenly swelled into a flood.

The reign of James I was strongly contrasted with the romantic excitement of Elizabethan times. A navy was built up under Elizabeth, but the complete naval supremacy which would endure for centuries after her death was achieved by men like Francis Drake.

Drake made many voyages of piracy and exploration and as previously noted he was knighted for one of them. A rough diamond, set against suave courtiers like Raleigh, he did as much as anyone to ensure that by the time Raleigh's first successful colony was planted in America, the waters off its shores were virtually dominated by English naval power.

Drake's greatest voyage started in 1577, 11 years before the crippling of the Armada. It began in a vessel of 120 tons called *Pelican*. Accompanied by two smaller ships, the *Elizabeth* and the *Marigold*, he set sail across the Atlantic with orders from his queen that included not only 'singeing the King of Spain's beard' by raiding Spanish ports in America, but a trip through the treacherous Straits of Magellan to look for the mythical southland, the 'Terra Australis'. Mapmakers of the day had convinced themselves, and monarchs like Elizabeth, that a hugh continent existed stretching

N.S. de la Concepcion surrenders to Drake

up from—and the whole way around—the South Pole to within a short distance of Asia, South America and Africa. The strait that Magellan had found at the bottom end of South America was believed by many to separate that continent from 'Terra Australis'.

Magellan had been killed by natives in the Philippines and only one of his original five ships had got home by encircling the globe. No one had dared try again—until Drake. He changed his vessel's name *en route* to the *Golden Hind*, plundered a few treasure ships in the Atlantic, and then passed through the treacherous strait, noting that there was, as far as he could see, no 'Terra Australis'.

Drake then swung sharply north, up the coasts of Chile and Peru, and raided a group of Spanish ships laden to the gunwales with Inca silver. One of these, *N.S. de la Concepcion,* surrendered with its crew and a vast treasure. Drake finally reached England, having gone completely around the world.

This 'master thief of the Unknown World' became a source of inspiration to his admiring countrymen.

Coat of Arms of the
Virginia Company

James I, whose reign saw the beginnings of English colonization

The Colonization of Virginia

Elizabeth's reign came to a close without England owning a foot of land outside the British Isles. There were, however, good reasons; one was the way Elizabeth chose to make England great. She had set a pattern which would persist, with great profit to England, for nearly two centuries: the granting of royal patents to companies of private individuals, giving them the monopoly of trade in a particular area. These companies flourished, doing trade with Russia, Venice and Spain. Some, like the East India Company, eventually came to have their own private armies. But they were companies, not colonies, needing trade, not land.

This familiar pattern was followed in the reign of Elizabeth's successor, James I. In 1606 he chartered the Virginia Company, comprising two subsidiary groups, the London

The building of Jamestown

Virginia Company and the Plymouth Virginia Company. They were authorized to select territories for themselves between the 34th and 38th parallels in what are now North Carolina and Maine, the London Company taking the southern half, the Plymouth Company the northern.

The disasters of the two earlier expeditions had by now been forgotten. Men and money poured in, particularly into the London Company. By December 1606 its expedition was ready to sail; there were 120 men in three ships under the overall command of Captain Christopher Newport.

There were numerous delays but at last the expedition headed out to sea. In the spring of the following year, after a two-week search up and down his allotted stretch of American coast, Newport decreed that they would disembark on what appeared to be an island. It was in a river which he christened the James in honor of his monarch, and the settlement was to be known as Jamestown.

THE PORTRAICTUER OF CAPTAYNE IOHN SMITH ADMIRALL OF NEW ENGLAND

Captain John Smith

It was low, swampy, muddy, hot and unattractive. The land was heavily forested which made it difficult to cultivate, but one feature settled the matter for Captain Newport: it was easily defensible.

And so the first successful English colony was planted in North America. Once again, there were about a hundred colonists, exhausted from their voyage, but this time they formed a nucleus out of which America would grow.

'Now falleth every man to work', said Captain John Smith, a leader among the colonists, 'the council combine the fort, the rest cut down trees to make place to pitch their tents . . . some make gardens, some nets etc.' In fact before they even built their own homes, the party cut timber to be sent back and sold in London. There was an increasing shortage of wood in England at this time, making this an extremely valuable export.

The new colony had been given an enormous grant of land

by King James I. It included, north to south, more than the present state of Virginia—and to the west, everything, right up to the 'South Sea', the Pacific Ocean.

On board Captain Newport's vessel—Newport News, Virginia, was named after him—there was a sealed casket. As instructed before sailing, he opened it as he dropped anchor.

Inside was a complete set of laws for the new colony. There was also the list of seven names which would comprise the 'Board of Government'. This somewhat embarrassed Newport because the list could not be interfered with, and yet one of the new dignitaries, Captain John Smith, was, at that time, chained to a beam in the ship's hold.

Newport was forced to have Captain Smith unfastened and sent ashore. The fact that he was considered a trouble-maker and charged with mutiny had to be forgotten.

The colony was fortunate. Garrulous, forceful, with a great deal of common sense, John Smith was just the kind of man Virginia needed. Alone among all the men dumped on

Jamestown church as it is today

'Jamestown Island' he seemed to have had the power to get things done, the ability to command. Without him, Virginia would almost certainly have vanished like her predecessors.

Inside 12 hours there was a pitched battle with Indians which ended in a draw, no one being killed on either side. The Indian chiefs came forward to parley and to explain in sign language that earlier visitors of the same dress and complexion had attacked them. It was John Smith who put

New World produce: potatoes, corn and tobacco

their fears at rest and sent them away with a few glass beads. From that moment on, Smith was the acknowledged leader of the colony.

Captain Newport sailed for England in June, and immediately an atmosphere of gloom and despair descended on the colonists. In the swampy, malarial location, the temperature was rising daily. Rains fell suddenly and torrentially, to cease as suddenly, leaving the ground a quagmire. The investors of the Company had assured them they would have

a year's supply of food: they had enough for only four months. Unfortunately there was little incentive to adventurousness since everybody shared the Company profits, no matter how hard they worked. There seemed to be no springs of fresh water, so men became sich with dysentery, drinking the brackish water of the James River rather than digging wells.

Many of the colonists were either gentlemen or unambitious, and they sat around eating up precious rations, making occasional excursions into the countryside in the hope of finding treasure.

John Smith was the exception. He somehow got his resigned, despairing compatriots organized into hunting parties. He also got them to collect oysters from the shore and berries from the forest. He had them dig a well.

Even so, by the time Captain Newport returned that September with more settlers and a scanty supply of rations, only 46 of the first 105 colonist were still alive. To the dismay of the survivors, Newport also brought a peremptory demand from the share-

Women colonists arriving.

Above: An Indian woman
Below: Pocahontas

holders in London that something of value be sent back. The only thing of value in what seemed a God-forsaken country was timber; so the community, under Smith's direction, started cutting down more trees and loading them onto Newport's ship.

Many of the settlers died, some simply from starvation. At first it was all the regular shipments from England could do to keep the colony in existence. But gradually, cajoled by appeals on behalf of patriotism, religion and reward, nobles, merchants, and ordinary citizens invested in the enterprise and increasing numbers of people volunteered to sail.

The eventual success of the colony was assured when a settler, John Rolfe, discovered a way of curing tobacco so that it was pleasing to European palates.

Mr. and Mrs. Rolfe (an Indian girl called Pocahontas) retired to England. By this time John Smith had also returned and published a much disputed account of how this same Pocahontas had flung herself upon him as Indians were preparing to kill him. Some time later Smith visited Mrs. Rolfe, but she had no recollection of him at all.

The Establishment of the New England Colonies

In 1624 the Virginia Company gave up its charter. The tobacco planted had not yielded up the prosperity which would change the face of their dismal settlement. A rapid increase in the death rate and an Indian massacre in 1622, in which 357 settlers perished, were the final blows.

The Indian attack came with brutal lack of warning to the colony, which had been lulled by several years of peace. There was also a belief that the Indians could be converted to Christianity and passivity. This resulted in the settlement being less protected and more vulnerable to raids. Thus, with a greatly depleted population, Virginia now became a royal province and entered yet another stage of her stormy history.

The Company was bankrupt, and upon its dissolution it came under the direct authority of the crown. The change in status hardly interested the surviving inhabitants. Since its

Indians hollowing out a canoe in Virginia

first settlement, some 5,500 men, women and children had been shipped to Virginia. Of these, 4,000 perished on the journey or shortly after they got there, and 300 had returned home. The population stood at 1,200.

As previously mentioned, there were *two* companies chartered by King James in 1606 to colonize 'Virginia'. The one granted the north (up to present-day Maine) achieved nothing. The first detailed study of that area was made by men like John Smith, journeying up from Jamestown to look for fish and fur. Until Smith's arrival, it had been called 'North Virginia'. He named it 'New England' and in 1616 he produced a pamphlet on the subject, *A Description of New England*. It was bursting with fact as well as fancy, illustrated with drawings of savages, some less

Pilgrim settlers

probable than others, but showing very accurately, for example, the way some Indians made canoes by burning out the trunks of trees.

Superimposed on a fine map of 'New England' is the only known likeness of Smith himself: bearded, handsome and proud.

It was a fine, bold title, 'New England'. But in 1616, there was hardly an Englishman between Jamestown and the 45th parallel of latitude, which James had specified as the top of the area his two companies would share. Already, in fact, the French and the Dutch were claiming that everything from the 45th to the 41st parallel (from present-day Maine to present-day Manhattan) was divided between them.

It was not until four years later when the Pilgrim Fathers landed, with a real determination to stay, that New England really began to exist as a colony.

The Fathers came originally from in and around the pleasant English county of Nottinghamshire. They were 'Puritans', a strict, unyielding branch of the Protestant faith set apart from the Church of England. Some Puritans were anxious to reform the Church of England and to make it 'lower church' (i.e., get rid of 'popery'), preferring an organization of church councils (Presbyterianism) or a federation of independent churches (Congregational-ism).

The Pilgrim Fathers were a radical group, styling themselves 'Separatists'. For them, no amount of reform would

76

The *Mayflower,* which brought Pilgrims to New England in 1620

make the Church of England anything but distasteful, and they refused to attend. They were heavily fined for their beliefs and threatened with jail.

The Fathers fled to Holland in 1609 where, so they heard, any religious beliefs were tolerated. They were permitted to settle in Leyden, where they established a Congregational Church, but other troubles assailed them. The Dutch craftsmen's guilds, like óur own trade unions, made sure that foreigners got the better jobs. The Pilgrims, as they were now starting to call themselves, were only able to get badly paid manual jobs.

They also strongly objected to their children learning to speak fluent Dutch instead of English. This so distressed a few Pilgrims that they returned to England, vowing that 'life in an English jail be better than freedom in Holland'.

The leaders of the community thought long and hard over this. At last, they decided that the only solution would be emigration to the New World. There they could found their own colony and establish their own rules.

They were eventually granted a lease of land by the Virginia Company. A joint-stock company of merchants invested in the enterprise by contributing £ 7,000 to finance the proposed settlement.

After several delays, the *Mayflower* finally departed for Virginia in September 1620. The Pilgrims planned to land on the shores of Chesapeake Bay. There were 102 of them,

77

Signing the *'Mayflower* Compact'

men, women and children, in a boat about 100 feet long, with three masts and two decks. A tiny ship by today's standards, but fairly large for 1620.

It was a long, unpleasant voyage, but although there was much sickness and distress, they arrived in America with only one death among the company.

There were many differences between these people and those at Jamestown. The Pilgrims went in search of freedom and nothing more, while the Virginia colonists went for the most part to better themselves and become richer. Another important difference lies in the fact that the Pilgrims,

The Pilgrims land at Plymouth Rock

desperate as they were to escape, were sailing into the unknown with women and children, landing with them on an uninhabited and probably hostile shore. It says a great deal for the courage of the Pilgrim wives and mothers and for the determination of their men.

On November 11, 1620 they saw land and everyone crowded onto the upper deck, some scrambling into the rigging to see better. What they saw was a flat and unattractive land. Only then did they learn that the boat had been blown away from its target and that they were hundreds of miles north of Virginia. They ordered the captain to sail south but he refused.

For more than a month the *Mayflower* lay at anchor in the shelter of Cape Cod while parties landed each day. At last they settled on a site where the town of Plymouth, Massachusetts now stands, and men went ashore to build houses. Before the end of the year they had settled there, though the *Mayflower* stayed at anchor in the harbor until April 1621.

Before the colonists landed, they signed the 'Mayflower

New England fauna

Compact'. An accident of navigation had brought them outside the jurisdiction of the Virginia Company, and it was essential that they establish some form of government to take its place. They pledged themselves to 'Convenant and Combine ourselves together into a Civil Body Politic, for our better ordering and preservation.'

They had elected John Carver as their governor before they left England, but Carver died within the year, and the

Above: an early fort
Below: a settler's log cabin

A rattlesnake

remarkable William Bradford succeeded him. A born leader of men — who would be badly needed, just as John Smith was at Jamestown — he was a farmer's son from Yorkshire, who was self-educated and spoke Latin, Greek and Hebrew. A man of tremendous sincerity, all-round ability and drive, he was to remain governor for most of his life, being re-elected 30 times.

The period after their arrival was hard, with never enough food. 'It was winter', wrote William Bradford, 'and they that know the winters of that country know them to be sharp and violent, and subject to cruel and fierce storms, dangerous to travel to known places, much more to search an unknown coast. Besides, what could they see but a hideous and desolate wilderness, full of wild beasts and wild men? . . . If they looked behind them there was the mighty ocean which they had passed, and was now as a main bar and gulf to separate them from all the civil parts of the world.'

So far they had had little trouble with the Indians, but under Bradford's direction they prepared, gradually, to defend themselves if and when necessary.

Seventeenth-century guns

It was a hard winter, and the settlers proved to be very brave. By the time the *Mayflower* sailed off in April of 1621, only 50 from the original 102 colonists survived. There had been 18 wives—only 4 were left. The rest had succumbed to the harsh climate and the difficult conditions.

In the autumn of 1621 the colony's backers in England sent out a ship with 30 more settlers—but no food or provisions. The following spring an additional 65 colonists arrived, also without food. During that dreadful summer, as they waited for their crops to ripen, the settlement nearly succumbed, *en masse,* to starvation.

But they were God-fearing people and grateful for God's mercies, however slight. When their first small harvest had been collected, they gathered together in thanksgiving. There were prayers, of course, but the Pilgrims gratefully planned a large feast as well.

The first Thanksgiving

Here is how one of the colonists described it, and if one realizes when Edward Winslow writes 'fowl' he means turkey, we see the origin of today's annual celebration:

'Our harvest being gotten in, our Governor sent four men out fowling, so that we might after a special manner rejoice together, after we had gathered in the fruit of our labors. They four killed in one day as much fowl as served the company almost a week. At this time, among other recreations, we exercised our arms, many of the Indians coming among us, and with them their great King, Massasoit, with some 90 men, whom for three days we entertained and feasted, and they went out and killed five deer, which they brought to the plantation and bestowed on our Governor and upon the Captain and others.'

That was 1621. With some variations, Thanksgiving, greatest of American feast days, has been celebrated annually ever since.

Settlers in Massachusetts going to church

While celebrating their Thanksgiving feast, the Pilgrims realized that they could not rely on a good harvest every year. Using the plentiful supply of timber at their disposal, they began to build fishing boats and to learn to also depend on the sea, rather than just the land, for food.

The Pilgrim Fathers had at first agreed to an impossible system of communal ownership, which was to last, their backers decreed, for seven years. It meant that no one owned land; that whatever was produced went into a common fund, out of which families were fed and clothed (and the stay-at-home shareholders profited). One only has to look at more recent history, to see what difficulties this system presents — the lazy man getting the same reward as his hard-working brother. In this small, remote community feeling against this experimental plan grew so strong that in 1623 William Bradford divided the land among the families, making each man owner of his farm.

Though the London backers were highly displeased, there

was little they could do. Bradford paid them a lump sum of £1800 and declared the joint-stock principle over.

The Plymouth colony had other, self-inflicted, problems. Their religion made a mockery of private life: it was one's duty to spy on one's neighbor and check up on his behavior, and the punishments for swearing or drunkenness were extremely severe. Men and women had to dress in certain ways and cut their hair in certain ways or risk rebuke.

Though all the Pilgrims in the Plymouth colony were nominally Puritans, it would be wrong to say that all had braved the unknown for that reason. There was a depression in England and in a few cases this tipped the scale, even though a Pilgrim might not care to admit it. Strict Puritan rules began to chafe. Tempers grew short.

King James, anxious to receive what benefit might accrue from these pioneers, legalized their settlement. Interest in New England grew rapidly in the mother country. Other migrants prepared themselves to leave for the New World.

Arrival of a fleet of immigrants in Massachusetts Bay

The Plymouth colony set an example of courage and devotion to an ideal for all future Americans and though its real influence on America's history and life appears today to be slight, they have in fact left a lasting legacy of tolerance and justice. Nevertheless, the settlement did not produce many individuals of note: its population was always small (7,000 when it merged in 1691 with the Massachusetts Bay colony), and in those 71 years it produced only one outstanding man, Governor William Bradford.

Charles I became king of England in 1625. Four years later he granted a charter for the formation of the Massachusetts Bay Company. Those who planned to settle around that bay were Puritans like the Pilgrims, but this time very few were fleeing for religious reasons. These men were less bigoted and richer. They did not need to borrow their expenses from the London merchants for they had money of their own.

Companies, like the Virginia Company, usually kept their

John Winthrop, the governor of the Massachusetts Bay colony

shareholders, their headquarters—and their charter—in England, sending lesser men to the colony to make the profit. But with the Massachusetts Bay Company things changed. The new company set up their headquarters in Massachusetts and took their charter with them. They also took huge quantities of food, tools and furniture in 17 ships, together with nearly 1,000 settlers.

In that first year, 1629, 2,000 colonists moved in. As with the earlier Plymouth colony, they were fortunate in their governor, although John Winthrop was a different type of man than Plymouth's William Bradford. Winthrop was a Cambridge graduate, financially well off, over 40, and an attorney by profession.

As a puritan, Winthrop had a definite aim—to establish a community rather than a mere colony, where he and his fellow Puritans could make a new life for themselves.

After 13 years, the Massachusetts Bay colony had a population of 16,000, more than that of all other English

An Indian building a birchbark canoe

settlements in America.

What and where were these other settlements?

Virginia, far to the south, had started her settlement in 1620. First in 'New England' were the Pilgrims, the Plymouth colony. But the Massachusetts Bay colony came to have the strongest influence on the various splinter settlements.

A clergyman, Roger Williams, had begun what would soon be the State of Rhode Island. He had left England with the other Puritans in 1630. In the wilds of Massachusetts Bay he found that, though he deplored the Church of England, the Puritan Church angered him still more. He thundered, to those who would listen, that all religions, be they 'Turkish, Jewish, Paganish or Antichristian, must be tolerated.

Clearly Williams was a disrupting influence in Massachusetts, and he was ordered to be sent back to England. However, Williams escaped. He slipped quietly off to an Indian camp where he spent the winter of 1635 and where he was treated with kindness. He, in turn, paid them handsomely for a tract of land at Narragansett Bay, outside the jurisdiction of

Pelts

Massachusetts. He built houses on his estate while he lived with his Indian friends, noting their customs, their methods of making fire and sending signals with the smoke.

A few English friends now joined him. He had decided to call his settlement 'Providence', for it had saved him from the bleak alternatives of repression in England or in Massachusetts Bay. Here he and his friends could live as they liked. 'I desired' Williams wrote, 'it might be a shelter for persons distressed for conscience.'

Roger Williams had little intention, at this stage, of starting a rival colony. But many others followed him to his 'Providence Plantation', where they raised cattle and planted corn. Soon, other men of liberal persuasion followed his example and set up their own small groups in the region, at Portsmouth, Warwick and Newport. By 1644 the four communities were thriving.

Williams went back to England, where he had many friends, including the poet John Milton, and persuaded

Trappers: Indian and English

89

parliament to grant him a charter to link the four settlements together as 'Rhode Island'.

Although a loose federation, to start with, historically Rhode Island is important: it was a tolerant, wise democracy long before any other part of North America — and years before England became a true democracy. Fifty years after Rhode Island had abolished trials for witchcraft, unfortunate women were being put to death in Massachusetts and in Britain. Two hundred years after Rhode Island abolished imprisonment for debt, debtors were being flung into English jails.

The Reverend Thomas Hooker, the Reverend Samuel Stone, and the elected governor of Massachusetts Bay, John Hayne, marched cross-country in 1636 and deep into what is now Connecticut. The fertile valley of its great river was claimed by the Dutch, but they were unable to enforce their claims in the area. The New Englanders therefore started three towns, Hartford, Wethersfield and Windsor. Other settlers soon began flooding into the new settlements. Men came mainly for profit, intending either to exploit the fabulous Indian fur trade or to seize fertile land for themselves along the Connecticut River. By 1662 this settlement joined with New Haven and other coastal groups to become the colony of Connecticut.

Several small separate groups had begun to inhabit what is now New Hampshire. Some believed themselves victims of religious persecution in Massachusetts Bay or England, others did not. Because there was no unifying ideal behind the settlements spread inside this large area, Massachusetts Bay claimed it as her own. Not until 1679 did New Hampshire succeed in breaking away. Only a few Englishmen were settled in what is now Maine, as the French held most of the area.

So much then for New England, a cluster of hardy, swelling communities, most of which had been started by religious persecution. Men might object vociferously to the way their God was worshipped elsewhere, sometimes only a mile or two

Launching the first ship built in America

away, but the freedom to worship as they themselves wished held New England together through that first half century.

On July 4, 1631, John Winthrop, the governor of Massachusetts Bay, launched the first sea-going vessel to be built in the colony. It was named *The Blessing of the Bay* and it weighed 30 tons. From that day on New Englanders built their own ships. Their trade with Europe, the West Indies and Africa grew yearly. Their climate might have been unkind for part of the year, but their seas were full of fish and their forests full of timber. They also kept thousands of acorn-fed hogs together with various other animals whose fur or flesh was valuable. The New Englanders were proud of themselves and with justification. They were getting richer, bigger and stronger every day.

They also kept their eyes on the future. It was decreed that for every 50 householders there should be a schoolmaster; for every 100, a grammar school. And in 1636 they established the first college—primarily for training Puritan preachers. Harvard University soon became one of the finest universities in the world.

By 1643, mounting conflicts with the Dutch in Connecticut, the French to the north and the Indians practically everywhere drove the New Englanders into seeking some form of mutual defense. Massachusetts Bay took charge. Representatives of four settlements signed the articles for a 'New England Confederation'. At the insistence of Massachusetts, the heretics of Rhode Island were excluded, but Plymouth, Connecticut and New Haven joined the Bay colony in a tight alliance designed to provide frontier protection to adjust boundary disputes and to further their mutual interests. By 1675, however, the Confederation had become useless, and the New Englanders were faced with some very difficult years defending their settlements.

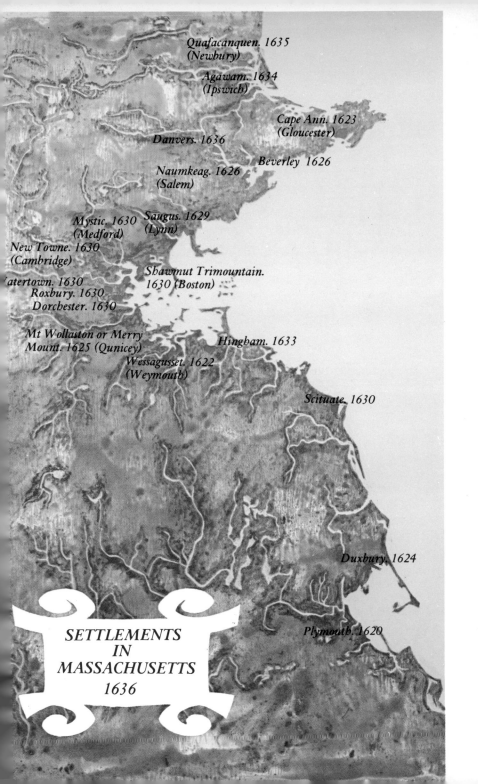

Quafacanquen. 1635
(Newbury)

Agawam. 1634
(Ipswich)

Cape Ann. 1623
(Gloucester)

Danvers. 1636

Beverley 1626

Naumkeag. 1626
(Salem)

Mystic. 1630
(Medford)

Saugus. 1629
(Lynn)

New Towne. 1630
(Cambridge)

Watertown. 1630
Roxbury. 1630
Dorchester. 1630

Shawmut Trimountain.
1630 (Boston)

Mt Wollaston or Merry
Mount. 1625 (Qunicey)

Hingham. 1633

Wessagusset. 1622
(Weymouth)

Scituate. 1630

Duxbury. 1624

Plymouth. 1620

SETTLEMENTS
IN
MASSACHUSETTS
1636

New Netherland and New York

In 1609 the Dutch, through the Dutch East India Company, sent a vessel to make yet another attempt to reach 'The Indies' across the Atlantic. Their aim, like that of so many seventeenth-century Europeans, was to find a northwest passage over the top of America, and like so many nations of that age, they employed a foreigner to do it for them. They engaged an Englishman, Henry Hudson, who sailed in the

Dutch map of 'New Netherland'

sturdy little *Half Moon.* Hudson discovered a river to which he gave his name, but he came back disappointed; however far up he sailed, there seemed no likelihood of reaching the Pacific Ocean.

Hudson had also tried further north, giving his name to a huge and treacherous bay, but it offered no westward route; the bay was a nightmare of floating ice.

For a while the Dutch were as disappointed as Hudson. They consoled themselves by claiming that all land on either side of the Hudson River was theirs and as this sort of claim could be stretched indefinitely, their claims stretched over

94

The *Half Moon*

territories covering the whole area between Virginia and New England. In 1614 the Dutch attempted to set up an armed trading post on the Hudson at Albany, but the venture failed.

By 1623, it was the Dutch *West* India Company which had taken an interest in the New World and which planned to colonize the Hudson River territory. As there seemed little enthusiasm in Holland for such a venture, the company issued a charter of 'Privileges and Exemptions for Patroons' declaring that any member who brought 50 adult settlers to the new colony inside four years would be given a large piece of land, and with it the title of 'Patroon'.

Even with this encouragement, the Dutch colony of 'New Netherland', as it styled itself, grew slowly. A few pioneers settled on Manhattan Island, a few more landed in small

Trading with friendly Indians

Above: early view of New Amsterdam
Below: Dutch settlers bowling

groups up the Hudson River as far north as Albany (which they called Fort Orange). In 1626 the Dutch West India Company purchased Manhattan Island from the Indians, establishing New Amsterdam at its tip. But there was still remarkably little enthusiasm in Holland about going there. The patroons worked hard at recruiting for their estates, pointing out that those who came to the New World would have cattle and tools supplied, as well as a house. They would also not have to pay taxes. However, no tenant could leave his patroon's estate inside of 10 years; each tenant would pay rent as well as a share of his profit; and each tenant would have to offer his crop first to his patroon, take the patroon's price as well as having his corn ground in the patroon's mill.

A tenant could bring an action against his patroon, but he would find to his dismay that the presiding magistrate

Women of New Amsterdam

was the same man. It was, in short, the feudalism of the Middle Ages resuscitated and brought over to the New World.

As an experiment it failed. There was too much good land available, and the tenants simply absconded. Thus there were soon Dutchmen settled throughout the eastern seaboard in small pockets, while the patroons found themselves with large estates which they were unable to cultivate.

The only part of this Dutch colonial venture that ever looked like succeeding was New Amsterdam on Manhattan Island. It attracted all kinds of people of all nationalities. In 1643 a visiting French priest noted that 18 languages were being spoken. One tends to think that the great racial mixture of New York (as New Amsterdam became) stems from nineteenth-century immigration, but 200 years before that there were Italians, Jews, Germans, Swedes, French, Spaniards and Turks.

It was a strange colony. Unlike the New England settlements and Virginia which had settled in and made plans for a long time, there was a strange air of makeshift about New Amsterdam. For many years a large part of the population lived in shacks, with beaver skins on top, drying in the sun.

The government in Holland was at least partly to blame, for it gave little support to a venture which seemed far less profitable to them than colonizing the Far East or plundering Spanish ships. Also the governors provided were, at least until the advent of Peter Stuyvesant, singularly incompetent. Wouter Van Twiller was a fool and a drunkard; Willem Kieft has gone down in history as the most murderous of settlers. Another Dutchman described a typical Kieft massacre: 'The Indian infants were torn from their mothers' breasts, and hacked to pieces in the presence of the parents, and the pieces thrown into the fire and in the water, and other sucklings were bound to small boards, and then cut, stuck and pierced, and miserably massacred in a manner to move a heart of stone.'

One-legged Peter Stuyvesant was appointed governor in 1647. He, too, left much to be desired as a leader, but he was certainly the most competent Holland produced. Under his choleric, despotic rule, order and discipline took the place of the chaos and drunkeness of the early years. Pictures still surviving of the period of Stuyvesant's governorship show pioneer women spinning peacefully, men bowling and clean Dutch interiors of the type that one associates with old Holland. Many of his people dislike him, but Stuyvesant, with his firm control over them, ensured that many pleasing Dutch characteristics would survive. Instead of shacks, firm dwellings with the distinctive sharp-stepped, gabled roofs became a part of the landscape. Unfortunately, Stuyvesant also made many enemies by his autocratic style of governing. One settler, Adriaen Van der Douck, headed a petition to the Dutch government in 1649, asking it to rule New Netherland from Holland and to set up schools, churches and some form of law and order in the colony.

But the colony's days were numbered. When Charles II returned to the English throne in the Restoration of 1660, there were only 10,000 white men in New Netherland, while New England boasted 50,000, Virginia 35,000 and Maryland

Peter Stuyvesant

Stuyvesant is persuaded to surrender to the English

15,000. In English eyes the Dutch now formed a tiresome wedge between New England and her other colonies. Had there been greater numbers of Dutch settlers, Holland might have withstood the English pressure, but small, defenseless groups are very apt to be 'liberated' for their own good. The English government decided that the New Netherland colony, by splitting their North American claims into two, was making commercial regulations hard to enforce.

So in 1662 Charles conferred on his younger brother, James, Duke of York, vast territories which included New Netherland, and the entire region between the Connecticut and Delaware Rivers, besides Nantucket, Long Island and a large part of the area that is now the State of Maine.

The Duke of York assembled a fleet with financial help from his brother. James did not sail with it himself, but appointed as deputy governor of his new domain a man called

Colonel Richard Nicolls. In fact, the Duke of York, later to be the last of the Stuart kings, never visited America himself.

The fleet sailed into New Amsterdam harbor on September 4, 1664, finding the Dutch completely unprepared. Stuyvesant tried in vain to rally his people. He ordered out all able-bodied men for a last ditch defense, hardly noticing that although they came, they demonstrated little martial spirit. Forty years of poor government, culminating in the religious bigotry of Stuyvesant himself, had sapped national pride. A letter arrived from Colonel Nicolls, assuring Stuyvesant that Dutch life and property would be protected if he surrendered. Although Stuyvesant pleaded with his subjects, he realized that there was no will to resist and New Amsterdam surrendered without a shot being fired.

In this peaceful, civilized way Dutch power in North

The English fort at New York. The original settlement in New York was a Dutch colony called New Amsterdam and was situated on the lower tip of Manhattan Island. But the Dutch were unable to meet the threat of the English, who sailed into the harbor of New Amsterdam in 1664 forcing the Dutch to capitulate. Except for a brief recapture by the Dutch (1673–74), it was to remain English until the American Revolution

America came to an end. The term 'New Netherland' was removed from the map, and the town of New Amsterdam was renamed New York.

Dutch influence on American life was slight, compared to that of the French, Spanish and English—and to that of, more recently, the other nationalities that have settled in the United States: the Italians, Poles, Scandinavians, Germans and Irish. A few great Dutch names survive like Vanderbilt and Roosevelt; there are still Dutch laws in New York State, but by and large, there is little trace of Dutch rule today.

In 1664, the Dutch in Holland may not have worried over much. For during that century they had laid the foundations of South Africa, driven the Portuguese out of Ceylon and discovered New Zealand. And at Batavia in Indonesia, they possessed at that time the largest commercial center in the Far East.

Governor Nicolls of New York was a tactful, competent

man, and the transition from Dutch rule to English was almost entirely without incident. He tactfully allowed Peter Stuyvesant to spend the rest of his life on a large farm situated where Fourteenth Street now stands. There was gradual English immigration so that the character of the port changed slowly, but then it had never been wholly Dutch: it stayed—as it was to remain—a town of many nationalities.

There were 10,000 white people in New Netherland when it fell to the English. Thirty years later, the province of New York—roughly the area of today's New York State—held three times that number. It had grown to resemble New England, with a thriving agriculture wedded to a fur trade and the bustling commerce of cities like Albany and New York rivaling that of Boston. People dressed, spoke and behaved as they did further north.

In considerable contrast was the rural character of the colonies further south, such as Maryland.

George Calvert, first Lord Baltimore, was the founder of Maryland

The Southern Colonies and Pennsylvania

The English Government hoped that one way of containing the Dutch was to grant nearby territory to Englishmen in the expectation that they would gradually squeeze the Dutch out. The Maryland Grant of 1632, of territory north of the Potomac River, reflected this policy, though as with other settlements there were other factors involved.

George Calvert had been a member of the Virginia Company as well as a favorite of King James I. Shortly before James died, he raised Calvert to the peerage as Lord Baltimore. He also agreed to Calvert's request for a grant of land in America and handed over, on paper, land stretching between the Potomac River and the 49th parallel. Calvert, a Catholic by conversion, intended to find a refuge for English Catholics in Newfoundland, as well as enriching his family.

With a king who had Catholic sympathies and a queen who belonged to the Catholic faith, English Catholics were not suffering persecution at that time. But memories were long and tolerance in England was comparatively recent. The Baltimores, while hoping to make a commercial success of their venture, also planned to make it a haven.

But when they actually arrived in Newfoundland they were sorely disappointed. What flowers could possibly bloom in a climate licked by an icy, savage wind from the North Pole? What man in his senses, persecuted or not, would choose to live there?

Celebrating the first Catholic
Mass in North America

Laying out Baltimore Town

His Lordship wrote plaintively to Charles I, pointing out that Newfoundland was uninhabitable and that he and some 40 other men whom he had taken with him were now sailing south. He hoped that Charles would give him a grant of land in Virginia.

Long before Charles' reply, Lord Baltimore had in fact reached Virginia and had been snubbed. The colony had not been started, like Massachusetts Bay, as a refuge from religious persecution, but it had strong ideas about religion and welcoming an influx of Catholics was not one of them.

His Lordship then returned to England and there persuaded Charles to give him the territory which is now the State of Maryland. Although they were not using this land, the inhabitants of Virginia complained bitterly: it had been included in their colony under the 1609 charter.

Charles ignored them and gave the requested charter to Cecilius Calvert, the second Lord Baltimore, in 1632. His father, George, had died suddenly at the age of 52 while the details were still being settled. He was believed to have succumbed to a weakness brought on by the climate of Newfoundland.

The second Lord Baltimore accepted the family's charter with gratitude. He informed the king that as the name 'Carolina' had already been chosen for another proposed settlement, he would call the new colony 'Crescentia'— the Land of Increase. The king, however, was adamant that Baltimore should call the colony Maryland after his queen.

Lord Baltimore could hardly object: his charter was unique, being virtually a title-deed for a vast private estate. He and his heirs could keep the place and either sell it or rent it. They could coin money, grant their own titles of nobility and devise their own laws. They could never be taxed by an English government. 'Maryland' it became.

The second Lord Baltimore in fact never went to America. He was proud of the acquisition and grateful that Catholics (if they wanted) could find a haven from persecution (when there was any), but he was not a pioneer like his father. The first expedition to Maryland was led by Cecilius' brother, Leonard Calvert, who became the first governor.

'Twenty gentlemen, with 200 laboring men' comprised

Above: William Penn
Below: Quakers

the first shipment to what was in effect a constitutional monarchy. The Baltimores had as much power in Maryland as the king enjoyed in England.

The idea of a Catholic haven gradually evaporated over the years, for the simple reason that Catholics showed less interest in getting to America than did Protestants. King Charles was executed in 1649 by the Puritans, and Lord Baltimore wisely appointed a Protestant governor. He and his family remained Catholic, but it seemed more politically sound that the family estates across the ocean should be governed by the majority party.

Then, when it seemed as if the Catholic minority in Maryland might be persecuted by the growing Protestant majority, the celebrated Toleration Act was passed by the colonial assembly in 1649.

Five years later the Act was amended to penalize all but the Puritans. Three years after that, this quaint piece of all-purpose legislation was restored to its original form.

The Baltimore family tried hard to build up numbers in their settlement, as well as keeping the original aristo-

Penn's ship *Welcome*

cratic flavor. They even circulated literature in England, extoling its charms. Settlers trickled in, slowly altering the colony's character. Like settlers elsewhere, these newcomers believed strongly in personal liberty and the right to participate in government. The Baltimore family gradually learned the hard facts of colonial experience—it was impossible to recreate a feudal atmosphere in the new American territories.

Maryland followed in the footsteps of Virginia, a colony devoted to agriculture, with a dominant class of great planters. By the end of the century both colonies had settled into the form they would retain until the Civil War. Planters with a rapidly increasing labor force of slaves held most of the power and all the best land. They built stately homes for themselves—like George Washington's Mount Vernon—and kept up social contacts with the world across the sea. Further inland were farmers with fewer or no slaves, who struggled in competition with the big proprietors. But in neither colony did a class of merchants develop: the Virginians and the Marylanders did their trading directly with England.

In 1660 England's monarchy was restored in the person of Charles II, and the new king found that he could lay claim to a large part of the east coast of America. He was generous, as

Above: a treaty belt

Right: an impoverished settler's home

already noted, for he gave New York to his brother James, and there were others who profited from this amiable weakness. He gave his friends, Lord John Berkeley and Sir George Carteret, a slice of what had been New Netherland, and they promptly christened it New Jersey, in recognition of the fact that Carteret had recently been governor of that island.

Berkeley's share of this handsome gift was known as West Jersey. A few years later he sold it to a member of the Society of Friends described by the historian Macaulay as 'a poor, shallow, half-crazed creature'. The Quakers were now in the business of colonizing.

William Penn was an Oxford graduate and the son of a distinguished English admiral. He became interested in Quaker ideas while still at the university and joined the sect formally in 1667 at the risk of being disinherited by his father. But Admiral Penn, conqueror of Jamaica and with influential friends at court, gradually accepted his son's decision, later leaving him a considerable fortune.

The admiral died, with the crown owing him £16,000. In consideration of this debt, Charles II gave Penn a part of the land which had been previously given to the Duke of York. In the whole history of colonial America no private individual was ever given greater opportunity in a territory known to be rich in natural resources. It was of this territory, on the western side of the Delaware River, that Penn was to write, 'God will bless and make it the seed of a nation'. The territory was given the name of Pennsylvania in 1681.

Penn came over to the new colony in 1682, his ship the *Welcome* carrying over 100 Quakers. They were fervently disliked by the other colonists with whom they came in contact, mainly for their pacifist sympathies. Nevertheless, the word got around that the new territory had opened 'an asylum to the good and the oppressed of every nation'. Like the Baltimores, but with more success, William Penn ad-

vertised all over Europe for colonists. Many who came were from Germany, the 'Deutsch', and their hardworking descendants are the 'Pennsylvania Dutch' of today.

The only thing the colony lacked was a port: the wheat that it began exporting to places like the West Indies had to be shipped down the river past Maryland. William Penn

Surveying the Mason-Dixon Line

managed to persuade Charles II to take land away from that colony and give it to him as 'Delaware'. The inhabitants and owners of Maryland were furious, but it was too late. Penn and his descendants were virtually owners of both Pennsylvania and Delaware until the War of Independence.

Many reasons have been given for the undoubted fact that the Quakers lived peacefully with their Indian neighbors. One false reason given is that they alone paid the Indians for their land. By then everyone paid for their land, however small the payment might have been. The true reason for Penn's success was that from the outset he had urged the settlers to be just in their dealings with the Indians. Of course, Penn fully intended to develop and sell sections of his new lands, enriching himself in the process. But he also had in mind the creation of a society firmly based on Christian ethics. And when Penn came to seek potential settlers for the new colony, this idealism and tolerance stood him in good stead.

The Boundary Stone today

With great honesty Penn tried to forestall over-optimism. He warned the first colonists that 'they must look for a Winter before a Summer comes; and they must be willing to be two or three years without some of the conveniences they enjoyed at home.'

And long after Penn's death there was still squabbling over the southern boundary of Pennsylvania, until it was eventually surveyed onto the maps as the 'Mason-Dixon Line'.

A less satisfactory colony was 'Carolina', scratched out on the map as far back as the time of Charles I. It was inhabited by a few wanderers from Virginia, until the 'Lords Proprietor' who had obtained a charter from the king sent out their expedition in 1670. It soon moved from the Ashley River to present-day Charleston, but its history was one of constant bickering, coupled with wars against both the Spanish and the Indians. It split into North and South Carolina, but by 1729 the crown had stepped in and repossessed both of them.

American or bald eagle
Daniel Boone, celebrated frontiersman
Gray squirrel

113

Above: Samuel de Champlain

Below: a French colonist wearing snowshoes

The Rise and Fall of New France

At this stage one should relate French activities during this period. They had involved themselves in the New World long before the English took an interest. It was a French king who had sent the Italian, Giovanni de Verrazano to look for a northwest passage to the Indies, and he had searched diligently the entire way from Newfoundland to North Carolina. Ten years later, in 1534, a Frenchman, Jacques Cartier, had begun exploring the St. Lawrence River. These were remarkable voyages, opening the way for large-scale French immigration in the years to come.

There was also, as previously noted, an ill-starred venture, near the future site of the Virginia colony, when Jean Ribaut tried to establish a French colony in 1562, but French interests soon centered themselves on the Gulf of St. Lawrence. It was from this northerly outpost that their most remarkable explorations were made.

Although it was gallant Jacques Cartier and his little flotilla of ships from St. Malo who discovered not only the St. Lawrence but Canada itself (and named it),

A beaver—much valued by trappers

the tale of Canada is inextricably woven into the biography of Samuel de Champlain.

Champlain was born 30 years after Cartier's great voyages, and like Sir Walter Raleigh, he was both a writer and a man of action. In 1603 Champlain made his first voyage to Canada, traveling far into territory which Cartier had already mapped. Then on a third voyage, in 1608, he founded Quebec, established good relations with the Indians of the neighborhood, and set up a highly prosperous fur trade. Though neither the French nor the English were aware of it at the time, the founding of Quebec proved to be a turning point in the history of North America, comparable to the founding of Jamestown in 1607. For it was from then onward that French Canada began to be a formidable rival to British interests in North America.

Fishing through the ice

Champlain's sketch of a fight with Iroquois Indians

It was Champlain's policy to make alliances with the Indians and for the most part these were highly successful. As there was open warfare between the tribes, he had to use tact and discretion in choosing the ones to befriend. The best furs came from north of the St. Lawrence River, rather than the south, so he became friendly with the Hurons who lived in the north.

Soon he was deeply involved in the cares and problems of Quebec and this put a halt to further exploration. There was no time to waste, though, in finding out everything about Canada, the 'New France', and he sent men out into the wilderness to live with the Indians and learn their languages.

The Niagara Falls, dividing Canada and the United States

THE ROUTES OF
SAMUEL DE CHAMPLAIN

MONTAGNAIS

Quebec

OTAGUOTTONEMANS

L. Nipissing

ALGONQUINS

Battle 1610

La Mer
Douce
(Georgian
Bay)   HURONS

uron

L. Simcoe

Ottawa R.   Hochelaga
(Montreal)

St Lawrence R.

L. Champlain

Lake of the Entou Honorons
(L. Ontario)

IROQUOIS

Battle 1609

Battle 1615
ONANDAGAS

MOHAWKS

Lake Erie

Map of Champlain's routes

Champlain himself stayed in Quebec, supervising the ambitious Winter Quarters which would ensure that for years to come Quebec would be French.

In 1613 Champlain found time to embark on a major expedition, up the Ottawa River as far as Allumette Lake. But he made his greatest exploration in 1615, traveling deep into the country of the Huron Indians, honoring his alliance with them and going to punish their enemies, the Iroquois. He wrote vivid sketches of what happened.

During the voyage Champlain mapped a portion of the unexplored Great Lakes. He was accompanied by intrepid Jesuit priests. Later on, some of them made remarkable voyages of exploration by themselves.

So far the three great colonial powers in America, the Spanish, French and English, had been uncompetitive, simply because the land area was so vast. But in 1673 the French launched a project which brought this peaceful period to an end. The civil governor of New France, Frontenac, ordered Louis Jolliet and the Jesuit, Jacques Marquette, to explore 'that great river which is called by the savages Mississippi and which leads to New Mexico'.

The Winter Quarters at Quebec

A. Stores	G. Galleries	O. Garden
B. Pigeonry	H. Chaplain's Quarters	P. Kitchen
C. Armory	I. Door and Drawbridge	Q. Slope to River
D. Men's Quarters	L. Walk all around	R. St. Lawrence
E. Sun Dial	M. Ditch all around	
F. Forge and Quarters	N. Gun Platforms	

The northern reaches of the river had been noted twice earlier by Frenchmen: first by Jean Nicolet, then by Father Claude Allouez in 1665, who had given a detailed description. The river flowed roughly south and might, the French reasoned, enter the sea off Florida or California. Their great hope was that its mouth opened out onto the Pacific. If they could but occupy the whole length of the river, down to the mouth, they would have power and influence eclipsing that of both the English and the Spanish.

It was a remarkable journey, proving that the Mississippi entered the Pacific Ocean not in California or Florida, but in the Gulf of Mexico. The French never reached the Pacific, but after their voyage there was no doubt where it lay. In 1682, La Salle reached salt water: a few years later the first French coastal settlement had been built to guard the mouth of the Mississippi.

The new region was warm and inviting. It had not been easy to persuade settlers to brave the climate of Canada; to 'Louisiana', which they named after French King Louis XIV men would flock in their thousands.

Having made their discovery and started a settlement, the French lost no time in protecting it. They soon built a coastal fort at Biloxi and planned others at Mobile, New Orleans and St. Louis. France had the Mississippi linking Canada to Louisiana, and she intended to hold all three.

Jolliet and Marquette had discovered the Missouri River during their explorations of 1673. From the angle at which it entered the Mississippi there now was a likelihood that it led to a northwest passage.

Unfortunately for France, these discoveries in America coincided roughly with the outbreak of war, caused chiefly by European fears of Louis XIV's aggressive policies. The French had recently inflicted punishment on the Iroquois Indians in the north and the Indians now elected to retaliate, with English encouragement. French Canada, flung into

Left: scalps
Right: the French explorer La Salle was murdered by his own men while trying to reach the mouth of the Mississippi in 1687

terror and confusion, began to fight back by sending mixed patrols of French and friendly Indians to harrass settlements in New England and New York. The English, in their turn, began to gain territory nearer and nearer to the Mississippi.

So, tragically for France, she began to lose grip of her northern and middle empire just as she established herself in the south. In Europe, one disastrous war followed another, with King Louis having ever-increasing trouble sparing troops for North America, and the English fighting harder on the principle that defeat in America would drag France to her knees in Europe.

A peace treaty was eventually signed in 1713—the Peace of Utrecht. By this time the English had helped themselves to what the French called 'Acadia' and which they now christened Nova Scotia. France had also signed over New-foundland and the Hudson Bay area as well.

In 1733 James Oglethorpe had settled Georgia at Savannah as a home for debtors, poor men and those suffering persecution. Although concerned with the slave trade himself, Oglethorpe decreed there would be no slavery in Georgia. But the colonists soon got around that prohibition, at the same time failing to achieve either the good life or the prosperity Oglethorpe had philanthropically planned for them.

Oglethorpe had made Georgia a British bastion, bringing

the local Indian tribes onto the English side. Not only did Georgia now threaten Spanish Florida, but it was a deadly threat to the French in Louisiana. Just by its position on the map, the colony gave promise of ultimate British domination over the whole area.

While this was going on, the European situation continued to be in a state of flux, though individual Frenchmen pressed on with exploration. Unorganized French parties pushed on into the southwest, while missionaries and explorers plodded westward. La Salle had returned to the New World and had been treacherously murdered by his own men, though this fact did little to discourage others. Few of them could have known that the days of New World France were numbered.

VEUE DE QUEBEC

Quebec from a map of 1729

It was the British prime minister, William Pitt, who was mainly responsible for the all-out attack on French North American interests. He had good reasons: the monopoly of the fur and fish trade had to be seized from France in order to weaken her; the American ports in which France had begun to build ships had to be captured, for the same reason. But the chief reason for fighting that Pitt advanced, was that 'the expulsion of the French would give security to British North American colonies'.

'I know', said Pitt, 'that I can save England, and that nobody else can.'

To this end he appointed an imaginative and energetic young commander, James Wolfe. Among other appointments was that of Captain James Cook, to survey the tricky St. Lawrence waterway prior to an attack on Quebec. Cook, of course, later became celebrated for his voyages beneath the equator, as well as for his exploration of New Zealand

Basilica in Quebec

and the East Australian coast.

The French, though they had constant trouble with the Iroquois, had far more Indian allies than the British. They could number Chippewas, Miamis, Potawatas, Hurons, Ottawas and Winnebagos among their friends; and these posed a considerable threat to any British attack.

James Cook had surveyed the approach to Quebec with such accuracy that Wolfe's massive British fleet had no difficulty in getting within sight of the place. The F.ench then sent out a squadron of fireships to destroy them, but this danger was boldly dealt with by British sailors in small boats, pushing the approaching, flaming vessels off into the shallow water where they ran aground and burnt themselves out.

A few warships got past Quebec's defenses, into the river upstream. Here there are cliffs which mount dizzily to a height of 200 feet. The brilliant French general, Montcalm, paid little attention to these vessels, for there was no way

General Wolfe dies as the British capture Quebec

by which they could bring fire to bear on him: his enemy was dead ahead in the Quebec Basin.

Darkness fell and the British began a barrage, with every ship in the Quebec Basin firing. Obviously a landing was intended and Montcalm prepared to repel it.

But at the same time, under cover of darkness, the few ships upstream of Quebec put troops into boats and rowed them silently to the shore. From the point at which they landed, a narrow track ran up to the so-called Plains of Abraham above, and British soldiers climbed up throughout that night.

By dawn of September 13, 1759 a large British force was in position exactly where Montcalm had least prepared for attack.

The battle was short and bloody. The French were decisively beaten, and both Wolfe and Montcalm were dead by the end of the day. The battle on the Plains of Abraham was perhaps the most significant in the history of North

America in that it precipitated the British capture and domination of all French Canada and therefore North America.

There was more fighting ahead, in many corners of the globe, before France admitted defeat in America. Then, a year after the fall of Quebec, the French Governor of Canada surrendered unconditionally to General Amherst at Montreal.

Three years later, in 1763, the war was finally over. Many strange things had happened. Canada, of course, was British, but so now was Florida, ceded by Spain in return for her own one-time possessions in the Caribbean. The French had given Louisiana to the Spanish, a gift which Spain was oddly reticent about accepting, so that French refugees from the north continued to pour in.

And Britain, the victor, now had an imperial realm, though she could soon count among her enemies not only the beaten European powers, but also a great many of her own North American colonists.

1. Massachusetts
2. New Hampshire
3. New York
4. Rhode Island
5. Connecticut
6. New Jersey
7. Pennsylvania
8. Delaware
9. Maryland
10. Virginia
11. North Carolina
12. South Carolina
13. Georgia

An eighteenth-century map of the state boundaries

Colonial Resistance to British Rule

The long war with France ended in 1763 and the British looked around with dismay. They had beaten France—but they were nearly bankrupt. The National Debt had doubled to over £130,000,000: taxes would be increased to regain some of the lost money.

Taxes, even before the French and Indian War, had taken 15 percent of an English landowner's income—a very high figure for the eighteenth century. Now, with prospect of this figure being doubled, British landowners and their government (virtually the same thing) began to ask whether the American colonies might not be invited to share the bill. Many of the colonists were in agreement; however, the British attitude toward the colonists was beginning to enrage their people. The British felt that the colonies existed only to enrich the motherland, supplying England with rice, cotton and sugar and buying English-made goods at high prices.

The thirteen colonies reacted strongly. They declared that most of them had been ruined by the war: they were fully as impoverished as Britain. Benjamin Franklin, a very great man but not always entirely truthful in matters close to his heart, was agent in London for Pennsylvania, and he declared hotly that his brother colonists were deep in debt and mortgaged to the hilt on Britain's behalf. Furthermore, they had furnished no less than 25,000 troops.

The truth, as historians now agree, was that in fact the colonists sent 10,000 troops to the front and profited considerably from the war. The British army had needed huge quantities of supplies and paid for them.

However, the British Government in the person of the prime minister, George Grenville, pressed doggedly on with its scheme of taxing distant colonists for benefits they were believed to have enjoyed. (No tax had ever before been levied upon America by Britain, only customs duties.) Grenville decided to levy a stamp tax, on the grounds that such a tax would fall only upon the rich. It would be similar to a tax which had long been operative in Britain, whereby all legal documents and publications required a revenue stamp. This would include land deeds, mortgages, licenses for taverns and many other documents. It would exclude

A handbill concerning the Stamp Act of 1765

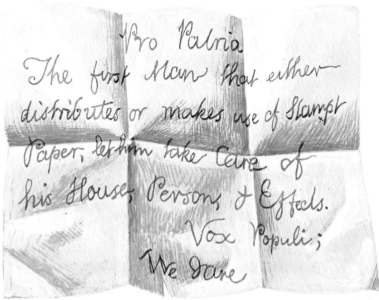

Molasses—obviously—began to be smuggled in. The British Government retaliated with Writs of Assistance which gave customs officers the right to search houses or ships for smuggled goods.

Once again rage mounted throughout the 13 colonies, and the first men to suffer from it were the unfortunate customs officers, closely followed by members of the staunchly loyalist Tory party. At first they were only hanged in effigy, but before long they were being beaten to death by mobs in the street.

It may well be that the Tories, numbering about a third of the colonists, deserved a large measure of blame for what ultimately happened. Many of them were wealthy, cultivated—and complacent.

General Gage, commander-in-chief of His Majesty's Forces in America, wrote to his government that a mere four British regiments could conquer the entire country. He greatly

A contemporary depiction of the Boston 'Massacre'

Drilling colonials

A Redcoat of
the Royal Fusiliers
7th Foot

underestimated the determination and strength of the colonists.

And so, in a weird kaleidoscope of misunderstanding, greed, righteous indignation, complacency and mob rule, the situation built up to a final crises. Parliament refused to concede the principle that they had no right to act on internal affairs in the colonies. In fact, by March of 1770 the only monies being levied from the American colonies were a duty on both tea and molasses (the latter had dropped from sixpence to a penny a gallon), but indignation still ran high. The tax on tea permitted the British-owned East India Company to sell tea in the colonies at a lower price than could the American merchants.

For many years British soldiers had been garrisoned in Boston. On March 5, 1770 a small group of 'redcoats' were attacked by a mob of 'liberty boys' shouting verbal insults and throwing snowballs and clubs; the British soldiers opened fire and killed four men.

This immediately became known as 'The Boston Massacre'. A terrible and totally disastrous deed, it instilled in the people of every colony a hatred for Britain. 'Remember the Boston Massacre!' became a byword for British autocracy.

In most quarters the Boston Massacre was played up for all it was worth. Paul Revere, a silversmith and engraver, produced a blood-curdling representation of the affair, printed in full color, which was seen in the farthest corners of each colony.

Even so, the next three years were a period of relative calm, though 'liberty' agitators still kept the general discontent alive.

During this period the East India Company, with its monopoly of all tea in the British Empire was in some distress, partly through the dishonesty of some of its officials, partly because American colonists were smuggling tea in to avoid taxes. In England, Lord North hit upon the scheme of allowing the Company to sell tea directly to America, in its own ships:

The Boston Tea Party

it need no longer sell it to middle-men at the London auctions. By this means, tea—even though taxed—could be sold on the shores of America for less than even the smugglers could get for it.

Not only were a great many people in the colonies involved in smuggling, but there were many honest men in America who simply disapproved, in principle, of a tax on tea or anything else. The Tea Act of 1773 produced an immediate and violent reaction from the colonialists. Radical leaders successfully used the Act to arouse public opinion throughout America against British oppression. When three tea ships came into Boston harbor on December 16, 1773, Bostonians demanded that they should be sent home.

When the ships crews refused to leave, a group of Bostonians dressed themselves up as Indians and boarded the tea ships. They tossed tea overboard valued at £15,000, and with it any chance of a *rapprochement* between the two sides.

The 'Minutemen Stone' today

The American Revolution

The tea incident in Boston enraged the British at home, and the government tried to punish the colonists by issuing the 'Intolerable Acts', closing the port of Boston. Furthermore, parliament reduced the powers of local government in Massachusetts and substituted a provincial government of its own. The new governor, of all disastrous choices, was to be General Thomas Gage, lately commander-in-chief. By this move—so it appeared to the colonists—the British government announced its determination to use force.

Angrily, the colonies made plans to hold a congress in Philadelphia, and in the first week of September 1774, the delegates began to arrive.

The First Continental Congress was hardly a representative assembly, being more equivalent to today's American Senate or Britain's House of Lords. Even so, the radical delegates marginally outnumbered the moderates. The Congress *advised* (no more) a complete boycott of trade with Britain, a decision which astonished the British, as did the advice that colonies should arm themselves against any eventuality.

In April 1775 General Gage was informed that this colonial arming had gone as far as securing a large store of gunpowder at Concord, some 20 miles outside of Boston. He

A Minuteman and his wife

decided to secretly capture the supplies early on the morning of April 19, and he was foolish enough to think that a force of 1,000 Redcoats could get there during the night before the rebels could make a stand. Part of his plan was the capture of revolutionaries John Hancock and Samuel Adams on the way. They were staying with a friend in Lexington.

Gage might as well have shouted his intentions all over Boston, for every citizen knew about them before dusk. Paul Revere, the silversmith and engraver galloped out of Boston,

Paul Revere rides to warn the rebels

ahead of the Redcoats, banging on doors right across the countryside. Adams and Hancock made their escape from Lexington, while militia captains pulled on their clothes and ran out to assemble their men, the famous 'Minutemen'.

An hour after sunrise on April 19, the British force reached Lexington and found themselves confronting 50 Minutemen.

Someone gave an order to fire, and in the ensuing battle eight Minutemen were killed and the others withdrew. The British carried on to Concord and found that the powder had been removed.

At Concord Bridge the Redcoats met several hundred Minutemen. Taken by surprise, the British retreated to Boston. By evening the British had lost more than a third of their force, some 273 men; 93 colonists died fighting them.

Word of the battle spread, and colonial armed resistance

The Battle of Bunker Hill

began in earnest. Reinforcements from England arrived to join General Gage under Generals Clinton, Burgoyne and Howe.

The one move the English should have made was to fortify the hills on the Charlestown peninsula, across the Charles River from Boston, for the hills dominated the town. When they discovered, one morning, that the colonists had now done this, increasing alarm spread through their headquarters.

On June 17, 1775, 3,000 British troops were ferried across the Charles River under General Howe. The untrained American troops let them get to within 50 yards of their trenches on Bunker Hill, then opened up with a fire that cut the Redcoats to ribbons. Bravely, General Howe led two more attacks in person. The third one captured the American trenches after the colonists had fired off all their bullets.

It was a bloody battle, with over 1,500 British and 140 Americans killed or wounded. It was also a battle that need never have been fought, for the British could have cut off the

George Washington in front of Mount Vernon

rebels' positions in the hills from behind and starved the colonists out.

Meanwhile, the Second Continental Congress was in session, and even before Bunker Hill plans were being drawn up for a 'Continental Army'. In all the colonies there was one man supremely fitted to take command: Colonel George Washington of Virginia. He was a wealthy Virginia planter, who had seen action in the French and Indian War, and was well known throughout the colonies.

Washington rode hastily from Philadelphia to Cambridge where British-held Boston was being besieged. He arrived on July 2, 1775 and soon he wrote of the men under his command, 'Such a dearth of public spirit and want of virtue I never saw before'. His Continental Army consisted of little more than a New England Force around Boston, with the promise, as yet unfulfilled, of contingents from other colonies. It took Washington eight months to condition the men and create an efficient fighting force. He was so successful in this attempt the British realized they had no choice but to retreat.

The Continental Congress quickly began to build up a navy. One of those who distinguished himself in it was a Scot who had then been living in America for two years, John Paul Jones. Others came from farther afield to join the American forces, such as they were. One of these was a 19-year-old French aristocrat, the Marquis de Lafayette, who remains the symbol of the friendship that existed between America and France, even though his was a smaller contribution to victory than that of the less glamorous Rochambeau or de Grasse.

A year after Bunker Hill, Congress appointed a committee, headed by Thomas Jefferson, to draft a formal Declaration of Independence stating that the colonies are now part of a single, free and independent nation.

After agreeing with his colleagues on the committee about the main points to be covered, Jefferson was assigned the task of actually writing the document. It was signed by the Second Continental Congress on July 4, 1776, the most significant date in American history.

In England there was little enthusiasm for this new 'civil war' and 30,000 German mercenaries had to be hired to help

The Marquis de Lafayette

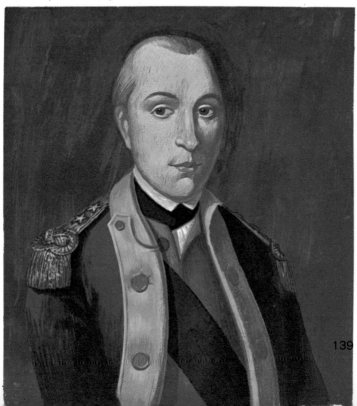

Cornwallis surrenders at Yorktown in the person of General O'Hara

in the fighting. Nobody believed they would be much use. In parliament there were many who hoped that a colonial victory would put an end to King George III's incompetent, unimaginative government.

After several defeats, General Washington's army had shrunk by the end of 1776, through lack of money and enthusiasm, to less than 5,000 men, a small percentage of the number he had commanded over 18 months before. There was also constant bickering among the newly independent American 'commonwealths' which led the British to believe that they were on the verge of a complete breakthrough and victory. However, General Burgoyne's disaster at Saratoga is fairly typical of British strategy in North America.

The plan was that a British force would start south from Canada, under 'Gentleman Johnny' Burgoyne, and join up with another marching north from New York. The two forces would eventually meet near Albany, having cut the American forces and the colonies in half. It appeared a straight-

forward campaign: the fact that the British were unaccustomed to the American wilderness seemed unimportant.

Burgoyne set off with 10,000 British and German troops (Hessians) and a few dubious Indian allies. Almost immediately, the Indians absconded. At the same time, General Howe, ordered to give assistance to Burgoyne, made a bold and rash decision—he decided on his own to attack Philadelphia. He reasoned that, with the seat of the Continental Congress besieged, George Washington would have to rush every available man there to its defense, and that Burgoyne could march south unmolested.

Howe defeated Washington at the Battle of Brandywine on September 11, 1777, but Philadelphia was evacuated before the British arrived. Meanwhile the unfortunate Burgoyne had lost most of his wagons, artillery and many of his men in forest skirmishes, and was forced to surrender to the American general, Horatio Gates, at Saratoga, on October 17.

Howe, in his hollow capture of Philadelphia, had driven Washington's army into Valley Forge just at the start of the winter. They were ill-fed and badly clothed and rather than freeze or starve to death, some 3,000 of his 9,000 men crept into Philadelphia and surrendered.

At this point Britain was apparently winning the war. Only George Washington kept the revolutionary spirit alive, and even he could not stop Pennsylvanian farmers from selling their produce to the British for gold, while his own men starved.

The arrival of the French changed the war, and the course of history. Comte de Rochambeau occupied Newport in 1780. His soldiers were far superior to the rough American volunteers and they gave the colonists great confidence.

The British general, Cornwallis, then began an assault on the south. He moved through the Carolinas and into Virginia. Here, in Yorktown, he hoped to get support from the British Navy and re-establish contact with General Clinton in New York. These two generals commanded the main British forces

The signing of the Declaration of Independence, July 4, 1776

in America, one in the north at New York—the other in the south, now at Yorktown, Virginia. Washington pondered which force he and his new French allies should attack.

Yorktown appeared to be a strong defensive position, but it was also a bottleneck and a trap. This was where the French alliance paid dividends, for Admiral de Grasse's fleet off the West Indies was ready to link up with a land attack on Cornwallis. As the fleet sailed, American and French troops rushed south to make sure Cornwallis could not escape from the landward side.

Events now moved with incredible speed. The French fleet arriving from the West Indies beat the British fleet, thus blocking any sea escape by Cornwallis. On September 30, the combined American and French armies of 15,000 men (twice the size of the British army) attacked.

The British force fought bravely, but it was outnumbered and unable either to reinforce its sick and weary soldiers, or escape. On October 19, 1781 Cornwallis surrendered.

The defeat at Yorktown rang the death knell of British influence in this part of their empire.

Hamilton believed strongly in a firm government, protected from too much democratic meddling by the masses. Others like Thomas Jefferson opposed this, believing in a brand-new 'equality of economic opportunity'. In short, Hamilton wanted firm government by a well-informed few; Jefferson, as little government as possible, by the will of the people.

At last Hamilton got a report drafted, calling upon all states to send representatives to Philadelphia early in 1787. There they would debate urgent commercial matters as well as draw up a constitution for a Federal Government.

The representatives hammered out the terms of a Constitution during the summer. By September it was ready and approved. There would be a two-chamber system of Representatives and Senators, with one Chief Executive—a President—much as it is today. Many of the American people resented the idea of 'Federalism', preferring to remain independent states.

Washington holding the American Constitution

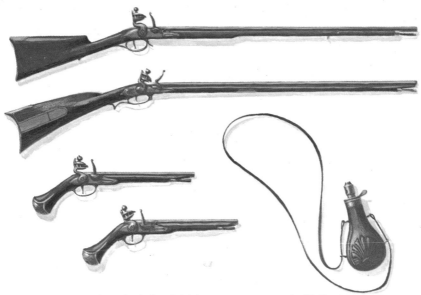

Every American had the right to carry arms: early flintlocks

But this idea was overruled and in mid-1788 the Constitution was declared law. Congress called for the election of a first President in February 1789, and George Washington was the unanimous choice of the electors. He was an older man now and he made a slow and dignified trip from his native Virginia to the temporary capital of the new United States located in New York City. After receiving a tumultuous welcome, Washington took the oath of office at his inauguration on April 30, 1789.

Surprisingly, perhaps, he invited both Hamilton and Jefferson into his Cabinet, although they had contrasting viewpoints. Ideologically, one can regard Alexander Hamilton as closely aligned to what became the Republican Party; Thomas Jefferson, on the other hand, supported many of the views later adopted by the Democratic Party.

Washington himself wished to retire at the end of his first four-year term. He looked forward to enjoying the peace and quiet of his Virginia estate and his fine house at Mount Vernon. After serving his country as its President for eight years, he refused a third term and retired into

Slave labor at a cotton plantation

private life. He was succeeded, as second President of the United States, by his Vice-President, John Adams, in 1796 and the seat of government was moved from New York to Philadelphia.

Washington had little time to enjoy his retirement. On December 14, 1799, just before the close of the eighteenth-century, he died at his home at the age of 67.

Just over a year later, a third President of the United States took office in the new capital city on the Potomac, named after America's first President. Jefferson was the first President to be chosen by a political party.

Curing tobacco

Tanning hides

What was it like, this fledgling United States, as a new century dawned? The population was still relatively small, but the people now had pride and were confident of the future. The census of 1800 revealed a population of over 5,300,000 (though a fifth of these were slaves). Populations had shifted since the early colonial days. No longer was Massachusetts the most densely populated: that honor now belonged to Virginia, with Pennsylvania second, New York third and Massachusetts in fourth place. It was still a largely agrarian country, prospering on crops of tobacco, cotton and cereals, and bolstered by profits from fish and fur.

Several serious mistakes had been made. Already farmers had found that their land wore out, and that though it might suffice for themselves, it was impoverished and almost useless for their sons. The pattern was an old one, copied inadvertently from the dawn of other, older countries. Intensive cropping, with no effort to maintain or increase the fertility of the soil, could and did ruin a farm within one generation. The great move westward, hardly yet beginning, would gain impetus from this fact: sons and daughters, if they were to live off the land, would be forced to emigrate to new territories.

At the end of the War of Independence, American soldiers had been given land in lieu of money. Many of them chose to settle in the area of the Ohio Valley. A few years later

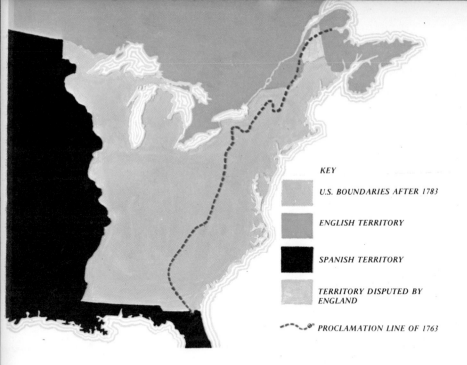

KEY

U.S. BOUNDARIES AFTER 1783

ENGLISH TERRITORY

SPANISH TERRITORY

TERRITORY DISPUTED BY ENGLAND

PROCLAMATION LINE OF 1763

Map of America after the Revolutionary War

the Northwest Ordinance Act of 1787 opened up a vast new territory north of the Ohio River, while government surveys and maps made it possible—and even safe—for a pioneer to buy land unseen, for as little as a dollar and a quarter an acre.

For those content to stay where they were, opportunities for enrichment were considerable: one did not have to travel many miles to find some new enterprise afoot: newly discovered minerals, new manufactures. And from the date of the Massachusetts School Law of 1647, opportunities for the education of one's children—if not of oneself—were at least as good as in England. This law ordered 'every township in this jurisdiction, after the Lord hath increased them in numbers to 50 householders' to provide a schoolmaster. After more householders had been produced by the Lord, they had to set up a grammar school. And, furthermore, 'if any town neglect the performance hereof above one year, every such town shall pay 5 pounds to the next school till they shall perform this order'.

That Act of 1647 laid the
foundations of a free school-
ing which was to be superior,
for many years, to that
obtained in England. Schoolhouses sprang up by the thou-
sand, and some of those eighteenth-century schoolhouses
—nearly all painted red—
are still in use today.

Although there were
plenty who wished to stay
stationary and reap the re-
wards of a settled life in a
land which was new enough
in all conscience to satisfy
the need for adventure, there
were others who did not. For
them, the 'conducted tours'
with pioneers like Daniel
Boone into incredibly fertile, virgin country like
Kentucky, were extremely
tempting. The spirit of
these people—we may al-
most call it the spirit of an
age—has been immortalized
in the famous statue of the
'Buckskin Man', staring
hard into the future.

Although she wrote these
following words in 1832, Mrs.
Frances Trollope's description of one side of American life is so accurate a description of the period that
they are well worth quoting.

The statue of the 'Buckskin Man'

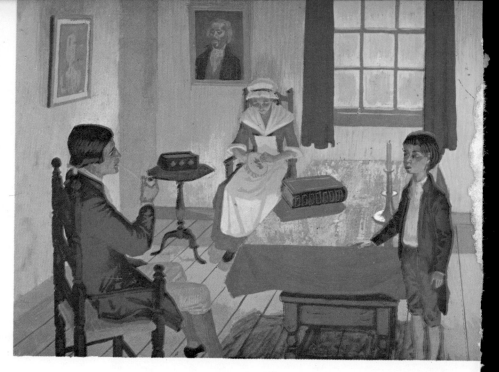

Interior of a New England home c. 1790

'The ordinary mode of living is abundant, but not delicate.
They consume an extraordinary quantity of bacon. Ham and
beef-steaks appear morning, noon and night. In eating, they
mix things together with the strangest incongruity imagin-
able. I have seen eggs and oysters eaten together; ham with
applesauce; beef-steak with stewed peaches; and salt fish
with onions. The bread is everywhere excellent, but they
rarely enjoy it themselves as they insist upon eating horrible
half-baked hot rolls both morning and evening.

'Almost every one drinks water at table, and by a strange
contradiction, in the country where hard drinking is more
prevalent than in any other, there is less wine taken at din-
ner; ladies rarely exceed one glass, and the majority of fe-
males never take any. In fact, the hard drinking, so univer-
sally acknowledged, does not take place at jovial dinners
but, to speak in plain English, in solitary dram-drinking.'

'Among the blacks I heard some good voices, singing in
tune; but I scarcely ever heard a white American, male or

female, go through an air without being out of tune before the end of it.'

Traveling by land was one of the hazards of American life at that time and most people tried to go by sea, lake or river. Using the waterways was not only less dangerous, but the journey often took only half the time. One Englishman wrote of traveling over land in America: 'To travel day after day, among trees a hundred feet high, is oppressive to a degree which those cannot conceive who had not experienced it.'

To cross the endless miles, men at first used pack horses. Soon the pack horses gave way to wagons, usually the Conestoga wagon, which was protected against the weather by a 'tent' of linen, stretched across a wooden frame. It was a lighter version of the Conestoga, the Prairie Schooner, which was soon to be used by many Americans to load up their homes during the first part of the nineteenth century and head West.

To realize the character and courage of the American people one only has to remember that only a generation after

The historic city of Williamsburg, Virginia is today a major tourist attraction

the first colonists had struggled to survive on the coasts of the New World, new waves of settlers staked their lives and futures to open up the other side of this vast continent.

Gradually roads were built, welding the states together so that individual settlements and towns eventually became a federal republic.

Nevertheless, shared hardships and improved communications cannot entirely explain how the peoples of the New World had became one nation. There was no unifying language, religion or laws to tie the French, Dutch, German and English settlers. Even so, it is evident that by the time of the American Revolution in 1776, the nation was already a separate entity. If there is one explanation of this, it lies in the common belief shared by all Americans, whatever their

OTHER TITLES IN THE SERIES

The GROSSET ALL-COLOR GUIDES provide a library of authoritative information for readers of all ages. Each comprehensive text with its specially designed illustrations yields a unique insight into a particular area of man's interests and culture.